THE
GUESS
WHOWHATWHEN&WHERE
PICTURE TRIVIA™
B O O K   S E R I E S

D1404324

Cutler, Dave.
    Movie edition / created by Dave Cutler.
    p. cm. — (Guess who, what, when & where picture
trivia book series ; 1)
    LCCN 2003115968
    ISBN 0-9742074-4-6

    1. Motion pictures—United States—Miscellanea.
I. Title.

PN1993.85.C88 2004   791.43'0973
                             QBI33-1752

© 2004 Picture Trivia IP, LLC.
Designed by Beth A. Crowell
Written by Tony Urgo
Edited by Joan Schweighardt

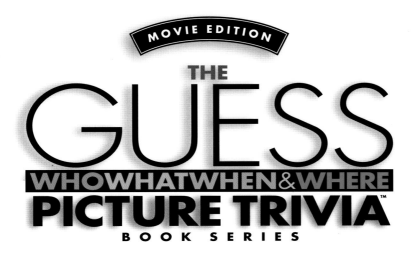

MOVIE EDITION

THE GUESS

WHOWHATWHEN&WHERE

PICTURE TRIVIA™

BOOK SERIES

CREATED BY DAVE CUTLER

GREYCORE PRESS

Dedicated to my wife, Carol, whose faith in me never ceases to amaze and inspire me.

The truth is I would not have been able to create this book if it had not been for the many wonderful and talented people who had faith in both me and this project. My sincerest gratitude to Tony, Beth, and Joan. You three are not only gifted professionals, but also good friends. Thank you for the many laughs and hand-holding. To Joe and Jerry, thank you for believing in me and becoming part of this special project. To Isaiah, Bob, Gail and Ron, thank you for your sincere advice and direction. To George and Bud, thank you both for your generosity. To Pam, thank you for sharing your talent with words. To Gilbert, Steve, Lane, Peter, Elizabeth, and everyone else at CDS, thank you for your valuable time, advice and support. You have been incredible. Finally, to the filmmakers whose art entertains our world, my sincerest appreciation and thanks. May you continue to provide us with memories forever. **DC**

Welcome

to the GUESS WHO WHAT WHEN & WHERE PICTURE TRIVIA BOOK SERIES.™ Picture Trivia is the new, fun way to discover what you really know about American pop culture (or to learn something you didn't know before!), using great visuals as your cue.

As you'll see, this colorful, captivating Movie Edition presents page after page of classic Hollywood eye-candy, each illuminated with insider movie lore and legend — fascinating for cinema fans at all levels.

We've designed it to be fun to read and easy to use. Just flip to any one of more than 150 memorable movie stills to challenge your memory with our Picture Trivia questions. (Keep those answers covered!)

Go a step further with our more difficult Bonus Trivia questions to see how much you really know about your favorite films. And prepare to be intrigued throughout by all of the little-known movie facts and tidbits you'll discover in the "About This Movie" section.

You'll also enjoy hours of entertainment with your friends! Flip the trivia page around completely to keep it hidden, hold the stills up for viewing, and let those questions fly. Keep score, pass the book around, and soon you'll know for certain who's the real GUESS WHO WHAT WHEN & WHERE PICTURE TRIVIA movie expert!

Now, get ready to learn the back stories ... share the gossip ... and see how much you really know. The GUESS WHO WHAT WHEN & WHERE PICTURE TRIVIA BOOK SERIES: MOVIE EDITION is your ticket to fun, insight, and endless entertainment.

Other editions of the GUESS WHO WHAT WHEN & WHERE PICTURE TRIVIA BOOK SERIES are coming soon! Look for them wherever books and gifts are sold.

Dim the lights,
　　　Butter the popcorn,

Roll the film...

PICTURETRIVIA

WHO WHAT WHEN & WHERE

5 POINTS per actor — **Who** are the actors in this film?

5 POINTS — **What** is the title of this film?

5 POINTS — **When** was this film released?

5 POINTS — **Who** is the director of this film?

BONUSTRIVIA

10 POINTS — What kind of snakes were in the Well of Souls?

10 POINTS — What did Marion call the inn she ran in Nepal?

10 POINTS — How high was the Staff of Ra?

ABOUT THIS MOVIE

The first full collaboration between two superstar filmmakers resulted in an unrivaled blockbuster that circled the world as certainly as the lead character himself did in the film. Tom Selleck was originally cast to play the lead, but then "Magnum P.I.," which Selleck had contracted to do, was sold as a TV series. Tom had to drop out, the actor who eventually played the part came in, and the rest, as they say, is history.

Answers • Who? Harrison Ford, Karen Allen **What?** Raiders of the Lost Ark **When?** 1981 **Who?** Steven Spielberg
Trivia answer 1 Asps
Trivia answer 2 The Raven
Trivia answer 3 About 72 inches, minus about a foot "to honor the Hebrew God whose Ark this is"

PICTURETRIVIA

WHO WHAT WHEN & WHERE

5 POINTS per actor — **Who** are the actors in this film?

5 POINTS — **What** is the title of this film?

5 POINTS — **When** was this film released?

5 POINTS — **Who** is the director of this film?

BONUSTRIVIA

10 POINTS — What kind of car did the title character drive?

10 POINTS — What was weird brother Dwayne's stated compulsion?

10 POINTS — What was the director's original title for the film? (It's a word that means the inability to feel pleasure.)

ABOUT THIS MOVIE

Until this film, a comedy hadn't won Best Picture Oscar since "It Happened One Night" in 1934. The original script had been written as a murder mystery (a story the writer/director/star would retool later for "Manhattan Murder Mystery") with a romantic story intertwined. Since the comedic elements were working so well, eventually the mystery elements were deleted and the romantic and comedic ones remained.

Answers • Who? Woody Allen, Diane Keaton **What?** Annie Hall **When?** 1977 **Who?** Woody Allen
Trivia answer 1 A VW Beetle convertible
Trivia answer 2 To swerve into oncoming traffic while driving
Trivia answer 3 Anhedonia

PICTURE TRIVIA

WHO WHAT WHEN & WHERE

5 POINTS per actor — **Who** are the actors in this film?

5 POINTS — **What** is the title of this film?

5 POINTS — **When** was this film released?

5 POINTS — **Who** is the director of this film?

BONUS TRIVIA

10 POINTS — What did the guys get together regularly at Oscar's place to do?

10 POINTS — What were the names of Oscar's and Felix's ex-wives?

10 POINTS — What hotel did Felix check into in order to check out through the window?

ABOUT THIS MOVIE

The two stars of this film had leading roles together in eight films — plus a number of smaller roles in other films, though not necessarily in the same scenes. One of them once even directed the other (in 1971's "Kotch"). These stars would repeat their most famous roles 30 years later in a sequel, possibly the longest stretch between sequels in movie history.

Answers • Who? Walter Matthau, Jack Lemmon **What?** The Odd Couple **When?** 1968 **Who?** Gene Saks
Trivia answer 1 Play poker
Trivia answer 2 Blanche and Frances
Trivia answer 3 The Hotel Flanders

PICTURE TRIVIA

WHO WHAT WHEN & WHERE

5 POINTS per actor — **Who** are the actors in this film?

5 POINTS — **What** is the title of this film?

5 POINTS — **When** was this film released?

5 POINTS — **Who** is the director of this film?

BONUS TRIVIA

10 POINTS — What were the names of the lead characters' husband and boyfriend?

10 POINTS — What destination did they decide they had to go to after the shooting?

10 POINTS — What classic car did they use on their road trip?

ABOUT THIS MOVIE

An unusual blend of studio-backed commercial film and cult hit, this film remains remarkable for its portrayal of two women whose plans for a road trip turn deadly and tragic. Originally envisioned with a low budget and with the screenwriter also directing, the script attracted enough attention to turn it into a big production with a veteran director. It became one of the biggest and most controversial successes of the year, provoking energetic debate on gender roles.

Answers • Who? Geena Davis, Susan Sarandon **What?** Thelma & Louise **When?** 1991 **Who?** Ridley Scott
Trivia answer 1 Darryl and Jimmy
Trivia answer 2 Mexico
Trivia answer 3 A 1966 Ford Thunderbird

PICTURE TRIVIA

WHO WHAT WHEN & WHERE

5 POINTS per actor — **Who** are the actors in this film?

5 POINTS — **What** is the title of this film?

5 POINTS — **When** was this film released?

5 POINTS — **Who** is the director of this film?

BONUS TRIVIA

10 POINTS — What was the first "specialty item" Andy requested from Red?

10 POINTS — What did Brooks Hatlen carve into the wood of the arch from which he hanged himself?

10 POINTS — What were the two things Warden Norton said he believed in?

ABOUT THIS MOVIE

Parallels for this film can be seen in other classic prisoner escape stories, including Alexandre Dumas' "The Count of Monte Cristo" and "The Great Escape." The director went on to film another prison-themed movie based on a Stephen King novel, "The Green Mile."

Answers • Who? Morgan Freeman, Tim Robbins **What?** The Shawshank Redemption **When?** 1994 **Who?** Frank Darabont
Trivia answer 1 A rock hammer
Trivia answer 2 "Brooks was here"
Trivia answer 3 Discipline and the Bible

PICTURE TRIVIA

WHO WHAT WHEN & WHERE

5 POINTS per actor — **Who** are the actors in this film?

5 POINTS — **What** is the title of this film?

5 POINTS — **When** was this film released?

5 POINTS — **Who** is the director of this film?

BONUS TRIVIA

10 POINTS — What word did Danny write backwards on the door of his mother's bedroom?

10 POINTS — What was Jack Torrance typing over and over all that time?

10 POINTS — What was the number of the hotel room that was off limits?

ABOUT THIS MOVIE

The director's penchant for filming an extraordinary number of takes per shot was in full force here, with over 120 takes for certain scenes. The exterior of the hotel was a real hotel on Mt. Hood in Oregon, while all the interiors—including the snow-bound hedge maze at the film's climax—were sets constructed and filmed at Elstree Studios outside of London.

Answers • Who? Jack Nicholson **What?** The Shining **When?** 1980 **Who?** Stanley Kubrick
Trivia answer 1 Murder (Redrum)
Trivia answer 2 "All work and no play makes Jack a dull boy"
Trivia answer 3 237 (It was 217 in the book)

PICTURE TRIVIA

WHO WHAT WHEN & WHERE

5 POINTS per actor — **Who** are the actors in this film?

5 POINTS — **What** is the title of this film?

5 POINTS — **When** was this film released?

5 POINTS — **Who** is the director of this film?

BONUS TRIVIA

10 POINTS — Who was Sam Spade's partner?

10 POINTS — How much did Joel Cairo initially offer Spade for a "certain ornament" in the form of a bird?

10 POINTS — What metal was the fake "gold" falcon really made from?

ABOUT THIS MOVIE

Already filmed twice before, Dashiell Hammett's classic murder mystery struck gold the third time around to become the standard against which all other private eye stories would be measured. Hammett had worked as an "operative" for the Pinkerton Detective Agency before he turned to writing; the highly eccentric and colorful characters in this story were inspired by people he met during his gumshoe days.

Answers • Who? Elisha Cook Jr., Sydney Greenstreet, Humphrey Bogart, Mary Astor **What?** The Maltese Falcon **When?** 1941 **Who?** John Huston
Trivia answer 1 Miles Archer
Trivia answer 2 $5,000
Trivia answer 3 Lead

PICTURE TRIVIA

WHO WHAT WHEN & WHERE

5 POINTS per actor — **Who** are the actors in this film?

5 POINTS — **What** is the title of this film?

5 POINTS — **When** was this film released?

5 POINTS — **Who** is the director of this film?

BONUS TRIVIA

10 POINTS — What was the name of the operation?

10 POINTS — How many of the dozen convicts survived?

10 POINTS — How many separate steps were in the plan to attack the chateau?

ABOUT THIS MOVIE

Though this is the story of a behind-the-lines assault on a Nazi-filled French chateau, shooting took place primarily in England. The grand set for the chateau was built so solidly and completely that it would have been too difficult to actually destroy; another "flimsier" one (a fake of a fake) had to be constructed out of weaker materials so that it could be blown up for the climax of the film.

Answers • Who? Charles Bronson, Lee Marvin, Donald Sutherland **What?** The Dirty Dozen **When?** 1967 **Who?** Robert Aldrich
Trivia answer 1 Project Amnesty
Trivia answer 2 Only one: Wladislaw
Trivia answer 3 16

26

PICTURE TRIVIA

5 POINTS per actor — **Who** are the actors in this film?

5 POINTS — **What** is the title of this film?

5 POINTS — **When** was this film released?

5 POINTS — **Who** is the director of this film?

BONUS TRIVIA

10 POINTS — What was the outcome of the match between the lead character and Apollo Creed?

10 POINTS — What was the lead character's morning drink before he went out running?

10 POINTS — What were the names of the lead character's two pet turtles and his goldfish?

ABOUT THIS MOVIE

It was this film that won the Best Picture Oscar in 1976 — America's bicentennial — beating "All The President's Men," "Bound For Glory," "Network," and "Taxi Driver," all films that explored different aspects of the American experience. Its nobody-to-somebody story did for its star what it did for its fictional character, against all the odds.

Answers • Who? Talia Shire, Sylvester Stallone **What?** Rocky **When?** 1976 **Who?** John Avildsen
Trivia answer 1 Apollo Creed won by a split decision
Trivia answer 2 Five raw eggs
Trivia answer 3 Cuff and Link were the turtles; the goldfish was Moby Dick

PICTURE TRIVIA

Who are the actors in this film?
5 POINTS per actor

What is the title of this film?
5 POINTS

When was this film released?
5 POINTS

Who is the director of this film?
5 POINTS

BONUS TRIVIA

10 POINTS — What classic rock song did the lead characters belt out in the "mirthmobile"?

10 POINTS — In what city and state did they live?

10 POINTS — To whose concert did they have backstage passes?

ABOUT THIS MOVIE

Before Austin Powers and Dr. Evil there was Wayne and Garth, one of the more successful "Saturday Night Live" sketches to be parlayed into a feature film. The stars of this comedy about a pair of friends with their own local public access show have indelibly made their mark on popular culture with the catchphrases "Excellent!" and "Party On!"

Answers • Who? Mike Myers, Claudia Schiffer (pictured), Dana Carvey **What?** Wayne's World **When?** 1992 **Who?** Penelope Spheeris
Trivia answer 1 "Bohemian Rhapsody" by Queen
Trivia answer 2 Aurora, Illinois — a suburb of Chicago (excellent!)
Trivia answer 3 Alice Cooper

PICTURE TRIVIA

WHO WHAT WHEN & WHERE

5 POINTS per actor — **Who** are the actors in this film?

5 POINTS — **What** is the title of this film?

5 POINTS — **When** was this film released?

5 POINTS — **Who** is the director of this film?

BONUS TRIVIA

10 POINTS — How much money did Peter offer Michael to change the baby's diaper even though it was Peter's turn?

10 POINTS — How did Jack meet Sylvia, Mary's mother?

10 POINTS — What were the professions of the three bachelors?

ABOUT THIS MOVIE

This director's first non-"Star Trek" movie was a commercial hit that established his reputation beyond Mr. Spock, and he joined other former television actors turned film directors, such as Ron Howard and Rob Reiner. This film was a remake of a French comedy, "3 Hommes Et Un Couffin," released only a couple years earlier.

Answers • Who? Steve Guttenberg, Tom Selleck, Ted Danson **What?** 3 Men and a Baby **When?** 1987 **Who?** Leonard Nimoy
Trivia answer 1 $1,000
Trivia answer 2 While performing together in a run of Shakespeare's "The Taming of the Shrew"
Trivia answer 3 Jack was an actor, Michael a cartoonist, and Peter an architect

PICTURE TRIVIA

WHO WHAT WHEN & WHERE

5 POINTS per actor — **Who** are the actors in this film?

5 POINTS — **What** is the title of this film?

5 POINTS — **When** was this film released?

5 POINTS — **Who** is the director of this film?

BONUS TRIVIA

10 POINTS — How many characters in the film existed only in the mind of John Nash?

10 POINTS — Which university did John Nash attend and later teach at?

10 POINTS — In what year did John Nash win the Nobel Prize?

ABOUT THIS MOVIE

This film took several liberties in the telling of the real life story of mathematician John Nash. Nash never saw imaginary people as depicted in the film; his hallucinations were strictly auditory. The Princeton tradition of giving an esteemed colleague your pen as a token of appreciation was fictional too. And Nash's Nobel speech in the film was not the one he actually gave.

Answers • Who? Russell Crowe, Ed Harris **What?** A Beautiful Mind **When?** 2001 **Who?** Ron Howard
Trivia answer 1 Three: the federal agent, his college roommate, and his college roommate's niece
Trivia answer 2 Princeton
Trivia answer 3 1994

PICTURE TRIVIA

WHO WHAT WHEN & WHERE

(5) POINTS per actor — **Who** are the actors in this film?

(5) POINTS — **What** is the title of this film?

(5) POINTS — **When** was this film released?

(5) POINTS — **Who** is the director of this film?

BONUS TRIVIA

10 POINTS — What were the names of the flight crew?

10 POINTS — Who did young Joey mistake the copilot for?

10 POINTS — Where did Ted first meet Elaine?

ABOUT THIS MOVIE

A spoof of many things, this film targets in particular a 1957 film called "Zero Hour!" and the later "Airport" series of films, some of which have dated badly as time has passed. The directing team pitched the idea of this film to the studio as "'Animal House' on a plane" in order to get interest in making it.

Answers • Who? Julie Hagerty, Lorna Patterson, Leslie Nielsen, Peter Graves **What?** Airplane! **When?** 1980 **Who?** Jim Abrahams, David Zucker, Jerry Zucker **Trivia answer 1** Captain Clarence Oveur, Roger Murdoch, and Victor Basta (For "Clearance," "Over," "Roger," and "Vector") **Trivia answer 2** Kareem Abdul-Jabbar (who actually played the copilot, Roger Murdoch) **Trivia answer 3** In a bar in Drambuie, off the Barbary Coast, while Ted was stationed in the Navy

PICTURE TRIVIA

WHO WHAT WHEN & WHERE

⑤ **Who** are the actors in this film?
POINTS per actor

⑤ **What** is the title of this film?
POINTS

⑤ **When** was this film released?
POINTS

⑤ **Who** is the director of this film?
POINTS

BONUS TRIVIA

10 What was the local watering hole where everyone congregated?
POINTS

10 What did the mystery woman apparently mouth silently to Curt through the car window?
POINTS

10 What did the license plate "THX138" on Milner's hot rod refer to?
POINTS

ABOUT THIS MOVIE

Seminal in many respects, this film had a troubled start and an unpromising future. Producer Francis Ford Coppola had to fight the studio to get the film released. It went on to launch the careers of the director and many of the cast, including Harrison Ford. The director became a millionaire with this film, which gave him the leverage and control to make his next one, a movie called "Star Wars."

Answers • Who? Bo Hopkins, Richard Dreyfuss **What?** American Graffiti **When?** 1973 **Who?** George Lucas
Trivia answer 1 Mel's drive-in
Trivia answer 2 "I love you"
Trivia answer 3 The director's first film, "THX-1138"

PICTURE TRIVIA

WHO WHAT WHEN & WHERE

5 POINTS per actor — **Who** are the actors in this film?

5 POINTS — **What** is the title of this film?

5 POINTS — **When** was this film released?

5 POINTS — **Who** is the director of this film?

BONUS TRIVIA

10 POINTS — In what part of the world was Zack brought up by his father?

10 POINTS — What was the term for the local women near the base?

10 POINTS — What did the initials "DOR" stand for?

ABOUT THIS MOVIE

The musical chairs of Hollywood helped the early career of this film's star when he took on roles in three films all originally offered to, but turned down by, fellow actor John Travolta: "Days of Heaven," "American Gigolo," and this one. Years later he did the same as Travolta when he passed on the starring role in "Die Hard," which then went to new action hero, Bruce Willis.

Answers • Who? Louis Gossett, Richard Gere **What?** An Officer and a Gentleman **When?** 1982 **Who?** Taylor Hackford
Trivia answer 1 The Philippines
Trivia answer 2 Puget Debs
Trivia answer 3 "Drop On Request," the term for voluntarily leaving Officer Candidate School

PICTURE TRIVIA

WHO WHAT WHEN & WHERE

5 POINTS per actor — **Who** are the actors in this film?

5 POINTS — **What** is the title of this film?

5 POINTS — **When** was this film released?

5 POINTS — **Who** is the director of this film?

BONUS TRIVIA

10 POINTS — Where did Madam Ruby the fortune teller say the stolen bicycle was hidden?

10 POINTS — What was the reward amount for information about the whereabouts of the bicycle?

10 POINTS — Where was the bicycle finally found?

ABOUT THIS MOVIE

After a number of very imaginative and clever short films and a stint as an animator at Disney, the director of this film hit paydirt in this collaboration with an equally quirky and imaginative star looking for a vehicle for his unique onscreen persona. The success of this film allowed the director to later make a number of more personal films, as well as the huge blockbuster "Batman."

Answers • **Who?** Pee-wee Herman (Paul Reubens) **What?** Pee-wee's Big Adventure **When?** 1985 **Who?** Tim Burton

Trivia answer 1 In the basement of the Alamo

Trivia answer 2 $10,000

Trivia answer 3 On the Warner Brothers studio lot, as a prop in a scene being filmed

PICTURETRIVIA

WHO WHAT WHEN & WHERE

(5) POINTS per actor **Who** are the actors in this film?

(5) POINTS **What** is the title of this film?

(5) POINTS **When** was this film released?

(5) POINTS **Who** is the director of this film?

BONUSTRIVIA

10 POINTS What were the two countries that went to war with each other?

10 POINTS What was Chicolini's job before Firefly appointed him Secretary of War?

10 POINTS What did Ambassador Trentino call Firefly, which led to war between their countries?

ABOUT THIS MOVIE

This was the last of the Marx Brothers' films to feature all four brothers (it was Zeppo's last appearance). The famous mirror scene, in which Firefly suspects it's not a mirror but someone pretending to be him, has been replicated several times, memorably in a Bugs Bunny cartoon, in an "I Love Lucy" episode, and as part of the opening credits for the TV series "The Patty Duke Show" in the Sixties.

Answers • Who? Harpo Marx, Chico Marx, Groucho Marx **What?** Duck Soup **When?** 1933 **Who?** Leo McCarey
Trivia answer 1 Freedonia and Sylvania
Trivia answer 2 Peanut vendor (and spy for Sylvania)
Trivia answer 3 An upstart

PICTURETRIVIA

WHO WHAT WHEN & WHERE

⑤ **Who** are the actors in this film?
POINTS per actor

⑤ **What** is the title of this film?
POINTS

⑤ **When** was this film released?
POINTS

⑤ **Who** is the director of this film?
POINTS

BONUSTRIVIA

10 Where was Cronauer
POINTS stationed before his transfer
to Saigon?

10 What did bar owner Jimmy
POINTS Wah call all American G.I.s?

10 What did Cronauer's
POINTS Vietnamese friend Tuan
turn out to be?

ABOUT THIS MOVIE

Though the original story for this film was co-written by the real Vietnam-era DJ Adrian Cronauer, ultimately the development of the script and the characterization by the star of the film bore scant resemblance to the real person and his experiences "in country." Nevertheless, the film was the surprise box office champ of the year, and for a few years following, it boosted the real Cronauer's popularity on the lecture circuit.

Answers • Who? Robin Williams **What?** Good Morning, Vietnam **When?** 1987 **Who?** Barry Levinson
Trivia answer 1 Crete
Trivia answer 2 Earl
Trivia answer 3 A VC (Viet Cong) terrorist

PICTURETRIVIA

WHOWHATWHEN&WHERE

5 POINTS per actor — **Who** are the actors in this film?

5 POINTS — **What** is the title of this film?

5 POINTS — **When** was this film released?

5 POINTS — **Who** is the director of this film?

BONUSTRIVIA

10 POINTS — What more legitimate lines of work was Bree trying to find?

10 POINTS — What was the standard charge for Bree's services, before anything additional was considered?

10 POINTS — For what was Bree criticized during the group fashion audition?

ABOUT THIS MOVIE

As much a character study as a missing person mystery, this film delved into the private and public life of a call girl trying to better herself through therapy and the pursuit of a better line of work. The star won her first of two Best Actress Oscars for this role, which was initially offered to Barbara Streisand.

Answers • Who? Jane Fonda, Donald Sutherland **What?** Klute **When?** 1971 **Who?** Alan J. Pakula
Trivia answer 1 Acting and modeling work
Trivia answer 2 $50
Trivia answer 3 Having funny hands

PICTURE TRIVIA

WHO WHAT WHEN & WHERE

5 POINTS per actor — **Who** are the actors in this film?

5 POINTS — **What** is the title of this film?

5 POINTS — **When** was this film released?

5 POINTS — **Who** is the director of this film?

BONUS TRIVIA

10 POINTS — What breakfast was Ted trying, with dubious success, to make for Billy the morning after Joanna left?

10 POINTS — How much did Joanna say she was making in her new job during the child custody hearing?

10 POINTS — What critical account did Ted just acquire, which needed his full attention at the ad agency?

ABOUT THIS MOVIE

Like many films that cast child actors in a critical role, the audition net was cast wide for the right boy to play the son of the two stars of this film. Justin Henry was only six years old when he made this film, and he is still the youngest actor to be nominated for an Academy Award. The male star won his first Oscar for his role of a divorced dad, after being nominated, but not winning, for more outsized roles in "The Graduate," "Midnight Cowboy," and "Lenny."

Answers • Who? Dustin Hoffman, Meryl Streep **What?** Kramer vs. Kramer **When?** 1979 **Who?** Robert Benton
Trivia answer 1 French toast
Trivia answer 2 $31,000 a year
Trivia answer 3 Mid-Atlantic Airlines

PICTURE TRIVIA

WHO WHAT WHEN & WHERE

⑤ **Who** are the actors in this film?
POINTS per actor

⑤ **What** is the title of this film?
POINTS

⑤ **When** was this film released?
POINTS

⑤ **Who** is the director of this film?
POINTS

BONUS TRIVIA

10 What can you buy in a
POINTS McDonald's in Paris that you
can't buy in a McDonald's in
the U.S.A.?

10 Who was the headwaiter at
POINTS Jackrabbit Slim's supposed to
be impersonating?

10 Who did Jules compare
POINTS himself to when talking to
Vincent about how he
wanted to "walk the earth"?

ABOUT THIS MOVIE

Featuring three major story lines intertwined and full of funny and fascinating details of character and dialogue, this film has become one of the most imitated, but seldom equaled, films of the Nineties. The director also beat the odds by not suffering a "sophomore slump" with this, his second film (the first was "Reservoir Dogs"), a fate many directors succumb to during the early part of their careers.

Answers • Who? Samuel L. Jackson, John Travolta, Harvey Keitel **What?** Pulp Fiction **When?** 1994 **Who?** Quentin Tarantino
Trivia answer 1 Beer
Trivia answer 2 Ed Sullivan
Trivia answer 3 Caine, in "Kung Fu"

PICTURE TRIVIA

WHO WHAT WHEN & WHERE

5 POINTS per actor — **Who** are the actors in this film?

5 POINTS — **What** is the title of this film?

5 POINTS — **When** was this film released?

5 POINTS — **Who** is the director of this film?

BONUS TRIVIA

10 POINTS — Which colleges were Oliver and Jenny attending?

10 POINTS — Who were Jenny's favorite musicians?

10 POINTS — What did Oliver's father expect Oliver to do after graduation?

ABOUT THIS MOVIE

A hugely successful hit in its time, this film made instant international stars of its two leads and garnered seven Academy Award nominations. Beau Bridges and Michael York both turned down the part of Oliver, while the director passed on "The Godfather" to work on this film.

Answers • Who? Ali MacGraw, Ryan O'Neal **What?** Love Story **When?** 1970 **Who?** Arthur Hiller
Trivia answer 1 Oliver was at Harvard, Jenny at Radcliffe
Trivia answer 2 Bach, Mozart, and the Beatles
Trivia answer 3 Attend law school

PICTURE TRIVIA

WHO WHAT WHEN & WHERE

🌀 **Who** are the actors in this film?
POINTS per actor

🌀 **What** is the title of this film?
POINTS

🌀 **When** was this film released?
POINTS

🌀 **Who** is the director of this film?
POINTS

BONUS TRIVIA

10 What car color indicated
POINTS that the person choosing it
was a genius?

10 What was the name of
POINTS Jack Byrnes' beloved cat?

10 What song's interpretation
POINTS did Jack and Greg disagree
on?

The class and culture clash between Greg and the world of the Byrnes family provided the veteran actor of "Taxi Driver" and "Raging Bull" with perhaps his best comedic performance, made all the more hilarious because of how straight he played his character, Jack Byrnes. A number of scenes were improvised between the two warring male leads, and three identical cats were actually used for Jack's adored pet during production.

Answers • Who? Ben Stiller, Teri Polo **What?** Meet the Parents **When?** 2000 **Who?** Jay Roach
Trivia answer 1 Green
Trivia answer 2 Jinx
Trivia answer 3 "Puff the Magic Dragon" by Peter, Paul, and Mary

PICTURE TRIVIA

WHO WHAT WHEN & WHERE

5 POINTS per actor — **Who** are the actors in this film?

5 POINTS — **What** is the title of this film?

5 POINTS — **When** was this film released?

5 POINTS — **Who** is the director of this film?

BONUS TRIVIA

10 POINTS — On which beach in Normandy did the soldiers land?

10 POINTS — What was Captain Miller's occupation before the war?

10 POINTS — How many brothers were killed before the decision was made to rescue the last one?

ABOUT THIS MOVIE

The coastline of Normandy today is far more developed than it was during the D-day invasion in 1944, so an isolated and barren stretch of coast in Ireland served as the Normandy beach in this film. The primary cast went through a ten-day equivalent of boot camp before filming began, while the cinematographer methodically removed contemporary coatings on the camera lenses to achieve the gritty, contrasty look effected by old newsreel cameras.

Answers • Who? Tom Sizemore, Tom Hanks **What?** Saving Private Ryan **When?** 1998 **Who?** Steven Spielberg
Trivia answer 1 Omaha Beach
Trivia answer 2 Schoolteacher (English Composition)
Trivia answer 3 Three: Sean, Peter, and Daniel Ryan

PICTURE TRIVIA

WHO WHAT WHEN & WHERE

5 POINTS per actor — **Who** are the actors in this film?

5 POINTS — **What** is the title of this film?

5 POINTS — **When** was this film released?

5 POINTS — **Who** is the director of this film?

BONUS TRIVIA

10 POINTS — How many notes made up the musical communication from the mothership?

10 POINTS — In what state was the Devil's Tower located?

10 POINTS — What was the name of the ship found in the middle of the Gobi desert?

ABOUT THIS MOVIE

This movie, coming right after the success of "Jaws," was another hit, propelling the director's reputation and career into the stratosphere. Innovative special effects, like injecting white paint into a temperature-controlled water tank to create clouds from which the UFOs could hide and reappear, were considered state-of-the-art in the pre-digital-effects age of film-making. Along with "Jaws" and George Lucas' "Star Wars," this film launched the blockbuster fantasy film era which continues to this day.

Answers • Who? Richard Dreyfuss **What?** Close Encounters of the Third Kind **When?** 1977 **Who?** Steven Spielberg
Trivia answer 1 Five
Trivia answer 2 Wyoming
Trivia answer 3 The Cotopaxi

PICTURE TRIVIA

WHO WHAT WHEN & WHERE

5 POINTS per actor — **Who** are the actors in this film?

5 POINTS — **What** is the title of this film?

5 POINTS — **When** was this film released?

5 POINTS — **Who** is the director of this film?

BONUS TRIVIA

10 POINTS — What arrangement did Jan make with Brad on how to share their party line?

10 POINTS — What were Jan's and Brad's professions?

10 POINTS — How many people did Jonathan tell Brad he was attacked by in the diner?

This film was the first of three successful teamings of the three major stars (the others were "Lover Come Back" and "Send Me No Flowers"). The studio was afraid the script was too racy for audiences of the time, but it became a well received, non-controversial hit. It was the first team-up of the then No.1 box office male and female stars. It was also the leading man's first full-out comedic role (after becoming famous as the rough and tumble "he-man" type).

Answers • Who? Doris Day, Rock Hudson **What?** Pillow Talk **When?** 1959 **Who?** Michael Gordon
Trivia answer 1 They split every hour of the day in two: Brad would have the phone from the hour to the half hour, and Jan would have it from the half hour to the hour
Trivia answer 2 Jan was an interior decorator; Brad a songwriter
Trivia answer 3 "Five or six ruffians" (but it was really only one person)

PICTURE TRIVIA

WHO WHAT WHEN & WHERE

⑤ **Who** are the actors in this film?
POINTS per actor

⑤ **What** is the title of this film?
POINTS

⑤ **When** was this film released?
POINTS

⑤ **Who** is the director of this film?
POINTS

BONUS TRIVIA

10 What was the make
POINTS and model of Cameron's
father's car?

10 For what was the real
POINTS "Abe Froman" (who Ferris
pretended to be at the
restaurant) renowned?

10 How many miles were on
POINTS the trip odometer after the
car-park guys were through
joyriding?

ABOUT THIS MOVIE

Near the end of this film, a big parade with people in German dress becomes the background for further hijinks of the main character. The event was actually the Von Steuben parade, an annual celebration in many cities, including Chicago, where this film took place.

Answers • Who? Matthew Broderick **What?** Ferris Bueller's Day Off **When?** 1986 **Who?** John Hughes
Trivia answer 1 1961 Ferrari 250 GT California
Trivia answer 2 Being the sausage king of Chicago
Trivia answer 3 301 miles (and 7/10ths, to be exact)

PICTURE TRIVIA

WHO WHAT WHEN & WHERE

5 POINTS per actor — **Who** are the actors in this film?

5 POINTS — **What** is the title of this film?

5 POINTS — **When** was this film released?

5 POINTS — **Who** is the director of this film?

BONUS TRIVIA

10 POINTS — What did Roger Murtaugh wish to do with help from the South African embassy?

10 POINTS — What "trick" enabled Riggs to wriggle out of strait jackets?

10 POINTS — What was the significance of Marty's gold pen?

ABOUT THIS MOVIE

A well known Los Angeles landmark house on stilts was fictionally destroyed in this film. To achieve the effect, two duplicates of the house were built: one on a sound stage for the interior scene, in which people inside were shaken and thrown around as the house began to collapse, and a second one outdoors, where several cameras caught its collapse and fall down the hill.

Answers • Who? Danny Glover, Mel Gibson **What?** Lethal Weapon 2 **When?** 1987 **Who?** Richard Donner
Trivia answer 1 To immigrate to South Africa
Trivia answer 2 He could dislocate his right shoulder at will
Trivia answer 3 He found it under the couch while on the floor grieving for his wife, who had just died in a car crash

PICTURETRIVIA

WHO WHAT WHEN & WHERE

5 POINTS per actor — **Who** are the actors in this film?

5 POINTS — **What** is the title of this film?

5 POINTS — **When** was this film released?

5 POINTS — **Who** is the director of this film?

BONUSTRIVIA

10 POINTS — How did Guy wind up getting the part in the play, originally given to another actor?

10 POINTS — What kind of dessert did Minnie make for her neighbors to "just try"?

10 POINTS — How much did Guy bet his wife that she was pregnant?

A B O U T   T H I S   M O V I E

This film is sprinkled with celebrity touches, in terms of people, places, and things. Even small supporting roles were filled with a venerable cast, including Ralph Bellamy, Sidney Blackmer, and Elisha Cook, Jr. In one scene Tony Curtis provides an unseen "voice cameo" on the telephone. The location of Rosemary and Guy's apartment was in the legendary Dakota on the upper west side of Manhattan.

Answers • Who? John Cassavetes, Mia Farrow **What?** Rosemary's Baby **When?** 1968 **Who?** Roman Polanski
Trivia answer 1 The actor who had originally gotten the part woke up one morning to discover he could no longer see
Trivia answer 2 Mousse (which Minnie called "mouse")
Trivia answer 3 A quarter

PICTURETRIVIA

WHO WHAT WHEN & WHERE

5 POINTS per actor **Who** are the actors in this film?

5 POINTS **What** is the title of this film?

5 POINTS **When** was this film released?

5 POINTS **Who** is the director of this film?

BONUSTRIVIA

10 POINTS
What did the rest of the family spend the entire story trying to persuade Clarence to do?

10 POINTS
What was Clarence's standard outburst when he encountered something he didn't like?

10 POINTS
What was the name of the family dog?

ABOUT THIS MOVIE

First a best-selling memoir and then a long-running Broadway play, the rights to this film cost the studio financing the project a million dollars — a record at the time. While veteran actors portrayed the mother and father, it also featured an early role with a 15-year-old Elizabeth Taylor as their daughter.

Answers • Who? William Powell, Irene Dunne **What?** Life With Father **When?** 1947 **Who?** Michael Curtiz
Trivia answer 1 Be baptized
Trivia answer 2 "Oh Gad!"
Trivia answer 3 Princess

PICTURE TRIVIA

(5) POINTS per actor — **Who** are the actors in this film?

(5) POINTS — **What** is the title of this film?

(5) POINTS — **When** was this film released?

(5) POINTS — **Who** is the director of this film?

BONUS TRIVIA

10 POINTS — What was the nickname Frank liked to be called?

10 POINTS — What did Frank at long last receive — but then reject — while in the hospital after being shot?

10 POINTS — What did "B.C.I." stand for?

ABOUT THIS MOVIE

This film was based on the true story of New York City's most famous police officer, who, by refusing payoffs endemic to the metropolitan police force at the time, became a lightning rod for political reform against vast city corruption. After playing one of the most well known fictional crime figures in "The Godfather" only a couple of years earlier, the star of this film turned his talents to playing an honest cop in New York City.

Answers • Who? Al Pacino, Tony Roberts **What?** Serpico **When?** 1973 **Who?** Sidney Lumet
Trivia answer 1 Paco
Trivia answer 2 A gold detective's shield
Trivia answer 3 Bureau of Criminal Identification

PICTURE TRIVIA

WHO WHAT WHEN & WHERE

5 POINTS per actor — **Who** are the actors in this film?

5 POINTS — **What** is the title of this film?

5 POINTS — **When** was this film released?

5 POINTS — **Who** is the director of this film?

BONUS TRIVIA

10 POINTS — Which movie prompted Annie's idea for meeting at the top of the Empire State Building in New York City?

10 POINTS — Which city did Sam and Jonah move away from after Maggie's death?

10 POINTS — What paper did Annie Reed work for?

ABOUT THIS MOVIE

In retrospect this film featured an inspired and commercially successful choice for its male and female leads: their lesser known first outing together ("Joe Versus the Volcano") was more of a critical success than a commercial one, but they hit it big again together five years later in their third teaming, "You've Got Mail."

Answers • **Who?** Meg Ryan, Rosie O'Donnell **What?** Sleepless in Seattle **When?** 1993 **Who?** Nora Ephron
Trivia answer 1 "An Affair to Remember"
Trivia answer 2 Chicago
Trivia answer 3 "The Baltimore Sun"

PICTURE TRIVIA

WHO WHAT WHEN & WHERE

5 POINTS per actor **Who** are the actors in this film?

5 POINTS **What** is the title of this film?

5 POINTS **When** was this film released?

5 POINTS **Who** is the director of this film?

BONUS TRIVIA

10 POINTS What did Aurora do to baby Emma in the crib to make sure she was breathing?

10 POINTS What did the doctor claim Aurora's real age was at her 50th birthday party?

10 POINTS What was Garrett Breedlove's one regret from his days as an astronaut?

Love it or hate it, this film elicited a wide range of emotional responses from the audience — often for the very same scenes. During its theatrical run, some couples could be seen exiting the theater with tears running uncontrollably down their faces; one husband, however, was heard telling his wife as the credits rolled, "I could've been home watching 'The Right Stuff.'"

Answers • Who? Jeff Daniels, Debra Winger, Shirley MacLaine, Danny De Vito **What?** Terms of Endearment **When?** 1983 **Who?** James L. Brooks
Trivia answer 1 Pinched her until she woke up and cried
Trivia answer 2 52
Trivia answer 3 None of the astronauts ever got together to compare notes about their experiences in space

PICTURE TRIVIA

WHO WHAT WHEN & WHERE

5 POINTS per actor **Who** are the actors in this film?

5 POINTS **What** is the title of this film?

5 POINTS **When** was this film released?

5 POINTS **Who** is the director of this film?

BONUS TRIVIA

10 POINTS At which year high school reunion did the lead character go through her time traveling experience?

10 POINTS What kind of car did her dad buy?

10 POINTS What did Richard call his concept of time travel?

ABOUT THIS MOVIE

In a period of fantasy filmmaking that contained increasingly spectacular special effects, this appealing time-travel story was done without any effects beyond the acting and the storytelling. The cast had to represent their characters from two different time periods and decades apart in age with only makeup and acting talent at their disposal. Look for the director's daughter Sofia and an early part for Jim Carrey.

Answers • Who? Nicolas Cage, Kathleen Turner **What?** Peggy Sue Got Married **When?** 1986 **Who?** Francis Ford Coppola
Trivia answer 1 Her 25th
Trivia answer 2 An Edsel
Trivia answer 3 Richard's Burrito (because he envisioned time folding over on itself)

PICTURE TRIVIA

WHO WHAT WHEN & WHERE

⑤ POINTS per actor — **Who** are the actors in this film?

⑤ POINTS — **What** is the title of this film?

⑤ POINTS — **When** was this film released?

⑤ POINTS — **Who** is the director of this film?

BONUS TRIVIA

10 POINTS — In what city did the story take place?

10 POINTS — On what topic did Eddie quiz his fiancée as a requisite to getting married?

10 POINTS — What was the big guy, Earl, trying to accomplish in the diner?

ABOUT THIS MOVIE

Drawing on his own childhood recollections and upbringing, the director of this film went on to make three more films ("Tin Men," "Avalon," and the most recent, "Liberty Heights") set in the same city, his home town. A number of characters show up again throughout the films in smaller roles.

Answers • Who? Timothy Daly, Steve Guttenberg, Daniel Stern **What?** Diner **When?** 1982 **Who?** Barry Levinson
Trivia answer 1 Baltimore
Trivia answer 2 Football
Trivia answer 3 Eating all the items listed on the left side of the menu

PICTURETRIVIA

Who are the actors in this film?
5 POINTS per actor

What is the title of this film?
5 POINTS

When was this film released?
5 POINTS

Who is the director of this film?
5 POINTS

BONUSTRIVIA

10 POINTS
What were the two lead characters' full names?

10 POINTS
In what state did the couple hide after the botched robbery in which they killed a man?

10 POINTS
What famous show tune was playing on the screen in the movie theater?

ABOUT THIS MOVIE

Two directors initially approached to make this film (which is now considered a distinctly American classic) were François Truffaut and Jean Luc Godard. The star, also acting as producer, negotiated an unprecedented 40 percent of the gross, and became very wealthy after the movie turned out to be one of the biggest hits of the year.

Answers • Who? Gene Hackman, Warren Beatty, Faye Dunaway **What?** Bonnie and Clyde **When?** 1967 **Who?** Arthur Penn
Trivia answer 1 Bonnie Parker and Clyde Barrow
Trivia answer 2 Missouri
Trivia answer 3 "We're In the Money"

PICTURE TRIVIA

WHO WHAT WHEN & WHERE

⑤ **Who** are the actors in this film?
POINTS per actor

⑤ **What** is the title of this film?
POINTS

⑤ **When** was this film released?
POINTS

⑤ **Who** is the director of this film?
POINTS

BONUS TRIVIA

10 On which California beach
POINTS did George and Tuna start
selling pot?

10 What was the deal George
POINTS made with his prison high
school diploma class?

10 How long did it take Derek
POINTS to sell the 50 kilos of cocaine
George provided him?

The director of this film died tragically of a heart attack during a celebrity basketball game in Los Angeles; a small amount of cocaine found in his bloodstream was determined to be a contributing factor to a death which has been ruled accidental. His death came less than a year after the release of the film, which is about the rise and fall of George Jung, master drug dealer.

Answers • Who? Johnny Depp, Penelope Cruz **What?** Blow **When?** 2001 **Who?** Ted Demme
Trivia answer 1 Manhattan Beach
Trivia answer 2 He would spend half the class teaching them the regular course and the other half teaching them how to smuggle drugs
Trivia answer 3 36 hours

PICTURE TRIVIA

5 POINTS per actor — **Who** are the actors in this film?

5 POINTS — **What** is the title of this film?

5 POINTS — **When** was this film released?

5 POINTS — **Who** is the director of this film?

BONUS TRIVIA

10 POINTS — How did Adam and Barbara Maitland meet their end?

10 POINTS — What was the title character's self-styled profession?

10 POINTS — What did the Maitlands have to do to contact him?

ABOUT THIS MOVIE

This film was the director's middle movie in a remarkable run of three hits in a row (coming after "Pee-wee's Big Adventure" and before the blockbuster 1989 version of "Batman"). The eccentric title character in this film gave the actor playing him great leeway to be comically outlandish and bizarre. A comic ghost story, it presents as one of its many memorable scenes a unique dinner table rendition of "Day-O."

Answers • Who? Alec Baldwin, Geena Davis **What?** Beetlejuice **When?** 1988 **Who?** Tim Burton
Trivia answer 1 After swerving their car to avoid a dog, they crashed through a covered bridge and plunged into the creek below and drowned
Trivia answer 2 Bio-exorcist
Trivia answer 3 Say his name three times

PICTURE TRIVIA

WHO WHAT WHEN & WHERE

⑤ POINTS per actor — **Who** are the actors in this film?

⑤ POINTS — **What** is the title of this film?

⑤ POINTS — **When** was this film released?

⑤ POINTS — **Who** is the director of this film?

BONUS TRIVIA

10 POINTS — What was Michael Gallagher's business?

10 POINTS — What newspaper did Megan work for?

10 POINTS — What was the name of Michael Gallagher's Prohibition-era wooden boat?

ABOUT THIS MOVIE

Controversial and provocative in 1981 but downright prescient today (considering recent faked story scandals at "The New Republic" and "The New York Times"), this movie was denounced by the newspaper establishment as a smear on journalists and their ethics. Ironically, the screenplay was written by Kurt Luedtke, a former reporter for "The Detroit Free Press."

Answers • Who? Paul Newman, Sally Field **What?** Absence of Malice **When?** 1981 **Who?** Sydney Pollack
Trivia answer 1 Wholesale liquor imports: "Gallagher Imports"
Trivia answer 2 "The Miami Standard"
Trivia answer 3 The Rum Runner

PICTURETRIVIA

(5) POINTS per actor — **Who** are the actors in this film?

(5) POINTS — **What** is the title of this film?

(5) POINTS — **When** was this film released?

(5) POINTS — **Who** is the director of this film?

BONUSTRIVIA

10 POINTS — How many "young ladies" were there all together?

10 POINTS — What was Walter "volunteered" to do by the Royal Navy during the war?

10 POINTS — What code name did Walter use when contacting Commander Houghton (aka "Big Bad Wolf")?

ABOUT THIS MOVIE

In this, his second to last film, the lead actor turned in a scruffy, cantankerous performance as an independent sailor imposed upon by a French teacher and a gaggle of schoolgirls. The film didn't do that well commercially, arguably because playing against his suave, urbane image after a lifelong career of glossy roles was a bit too far afield from audience expectations. It was the only part he ever played where he appeared unshaven on screen for the entire film.

Answers • Who? Leslie Caron, Cary Grant **What?** Father Goose **When?** 1964 **Who?** Ralph Nelson
Trivia answer 1 Seven
Trivia answer 2 To be a coast watcher/plane spotter
Trivia answer 3 "Mother Goose"

PICTURETRIVIA

WHO WHAT WHEN & WHERE

5 POINTS per actor — **Who** are the actors in this film?

5 POINTS — **What** is the title of this film?

5 POINTS — **When** was this film released?

5 POINTS — **Who** is the director of this film?

BONUSTRIVIA

10 POINTS — What were the three worlds that comprised the Delos amusement park?

10 POINTS — What prevented someone from shooting a real person in the park?

10 POINTS — What was the only visible body part that revealed that an individual was actually a robot?

ABOUT THIS MOVIE

Elements of this film presaged many ideas used in later films, from the theme resort used in "Jurassic Park," to the human-looking artificial intelligences of "Blade Runner" and "Terminator," and even to the idea of packaged experiences, like the false memories in "Total Recall" and the virtual experiences on the holodeck in "Star Trek."

Answers • Who? Yul Brynner, Richard Benjamin **What?** Westworld **When?** 1973 **Who?** Michael Crichton

Trivia answer 1 Medieval World, Roman World, and Westworld

Trivia answer 2 The guns contained sensing devices that prevented them from firing at any target with a body temperature

Trivia answer 3 The hands, which had raised ring formations circling the finger joints

PICTURE TRIVIA

WHO WHAT WHEN & WHERE

5 POINTS per actor — **Who** are the actors in this film?

5 POINTS — **What** is the title of this film?

5 POINTS — **When** was this film released?

5 POINTS — **Who** is the director of this film?

BONUS TRIVIA

10 POINTS — What kind of weapon did Callahan use?

10 POINTS — What was his title in the police department?

10 POINTS — What amount of money did the killer demand as extortion to stop his killings?

ABOUT THIS MOVIE

The star of this film took on this iconic role after the part was turned down by John Wayne, Steve McQueen, and Paul Newman. After the release and success of this film, John Wayne publicly regretted passing on the part.

Answers • Who? Clint Eastwood **What?** Dirty Harry **When?** 1972 **Who?** Don Siegel
Trivia answer 1 A .44 Magnum
Trivia answer 2 Inspector
Trivia answer 3 $100,000

PICTURETRIVIA

5 POINTS per actor — **Who** are the actors in this film?

5 POINTS — **What** is the title of this film?

5 POINTS — **When** was this film released?

5 POINTS — **Who** is the director of this film?

BONUSTRIVIA

10 POINTS — Why did Sean vow not to fight anyone again?

10 POINTS — What was the name of the town in Ireland that Sean Thornton returned to?

10 POINTS — How much was in Mary Kate's dowry at the wedding?

ABOUT THIS MOVIE

Despite the major stars committed to this film, it took the director 16 years to get the project off the ground. It was dismissed by studios as a "silly Irish love story" that wouldn't make any money. Filmed in early Technicolor at greater cost than in black & white, it went on to win Academy Awards for both the director and the cinematographer.

Answers • **Who?** Maureen O'Hara, John Wayne **What?** The Quiet Man **When?** 1952 **Who?** John Ford
Trivia answer 1 He killed a man in the ring when he was a professional boxer named "Trooper Thornton"
Trivia answer 2 Innisfree
Trivia answer 3 350 Irish pounds in gold

PICTURETRIVIA

WHO WHAT WHEN & WHERE

(5 POINTS per actor) **Who** are the actors in this film?

(5 POINTS) **What** is the title of this film?

(5 POINTS) **When** was this film released?

(5 POINTS) **Who** is the director of this film?

BONUSTRIVIA

10 POINTS What was mobster Siegel's real first name?

10 POINTS What was the name of the first casino he opened in Las Vegas?

10 POINTS How much did he pay for opera singer Lawrence Tibbett's Beverly Hills mansion?

ABOUT THIS MOVIE

Nearly a quarter of a century after playing bank robber Clyde Barrow in "Bonnie and Clyde" (1967), this film's leading man returned to the crime genre in the role of a much bigger gangster, building the first casino hotel in the then quiet desert community of Las Vegas. Larger than life characters—both real and imaginary—have become the lead actor's specialty, including American "Soviet" journalist John Reed and even legendary comic book hero Dick Tracy.

Answers • Who? Warren Beatty **What?** Bugsy **When?** 1991 **Who?** Barry Levinson
Trivia answer 1 Ben
Trivia answer 2 The Flamingo
Trivia answer 3 $60,000

PICTURE TRIVIA

WHO WHAT WHEN & WHERE

(5) POINTS per actor — **Who** are the actors in this film?

(5) POINTS — **What** is the title of this film?

(5) POINTS — **When** was this film released?

(5) POINTS — **Who** is the director of this film?

BONUS TRIVIA

10 POINTS — What two entities shared the same name?

10 POINTS — What was the loot that everyone was trying to get ahold of?

10 POINTS — Who was Otto's favorite philosopher?

ABOUT THIS MOVIE

The character Archie Leach was named after Cary Grant, who was born Archie Leach in the same town in England in which the star/writer of this film was born. This writer found a director for his script in a 78-year-old veteran, whose film career began in the 1940s with such classics as "The Lavender Hill Mob" and several episodes of the famed Sixties British television series "The Avengers" and "Danger Man" ("Secret Agent" in the U.S.).

Answers • Who? Kevin Kline, Jamie Lee Curtis, John Cleese **What?** A Fish Called Wanda **When?** 1988 **Who?** Charles Crichton
Trivia answer 1 A fish and Jamie Lee Curtis' character
Trivia answer 2 A stolen cache of diamonds
Trivia answer 3 Friedrich Nietzsche

PICTURE TRIVIA

WHO WHAT WHEN & WHERE

5 POINTS per actor — **Who** are the actors in this film?

5 POINTS — **What** is the title of this film?

5 POINTS — **When** was this film released?

5 POINTS — **Who** is the director of this film?

BONUS TRIVIA

10 POINTS — What was the nickname of the army pal who was the brother of the Haynes sisters?

10 POINTS — What was the name of the nightclub where Wallace and Davis met the Haynes sisters?

10 POINTS — What was the TV show Wallace appeared on?

ABOUT THIS MOVIE

A remake of an earlier film ("Holiday Inn"), the casting was planned to reunite the stars of the original film. But one of the stars, Fred Astaire, turned the part down, and it then went to Donald O'Connor, who later turned it down as well. The Astaire role finally went to this film's costar.

Answers • Who? Vera-Ellen, Danny Kaye, Rosemary Clooney, Bing Crosby **What?** White Christmas **When?** 1954 **Who?** Michael Curtiz

Trivia answer 1 Freckle-face Haynes, the dog-face boy

Trivia answer 2 Novello's

Trivia answer 3 "The Ed Harrison Show"

PICTURE TRIVIA

WHO WHAT WHEN & WHERE

(5) POINTS per actor — **Who** are the actors in this film?

(5) POINTS — **What** is the title of this film?

(5) POINTS — **When** was this film released?

(5) POINTS — **Who** is the director of this film?

BONUS TRIVIA

10 POINTS — What did the lead character name his shrimp boat?

10 POINTS — What company's stock did the lead character unknowingly own and unwittingly become wealthy from?

10 POINTS — What was the lead character's IQ according to his elementary school principle?

ABOUT THIS MOVIE

Undefinable as a movie in any category, this film broke all box office records and brought the star his second Oscar (he won the first the previous year for "Philadelphia"). Look for the small but crucial part of the main character's son, played by a very young Haley Joel Osment.

Answers • Who? Gary Sinise, Tom Hanks **What?** Forrest Gump **When?** 1994 **Who?** Robert Zemeckis
Trivia answer 1 Jenny
Trivia answer 2 Apple Computer
Trivia answer 3 75

PICTURE TRIVIA

WHO WHAT WHEN & WHERE

5 POINTS per actor — **Who** are the actors in this film?

5 POINTS — **What** is the title of this film?

5 POINTS — **When** was this film released?

5 POINTS — **Who** is the director of this film?

BONUS TRIVIA

10 POINTS — How did Brick injure his ankle?

10 POINTS — What birthday did Big Daddy celebrate upon his return home?

10 POINTS — What did Big Daddy inherit from his father?

ABOUT THIS MOVIE

Though a classic today, this film was made during the height of the Communist blacklistings and under the thumb of the Hollywood Production Code, so many elements of Tennessee Williams' original play had to be downplayed or completely deleted. Tennessee Williams loathed it: all the references to homosexuality were absent, and the ending was substantially changed.

Answers • Who? Burl Ives, Elizabeth Taylor, Paul Newman **What?** Cat on a Hot Tin Roof **When?** 1958 **Who?** Richard Brooks
Trivia answer 1 Trying to run the high hurdles in the middle of the night to relive his high school days
Trivia answer 2 His 65th
Trivia answer 3 A suitcase with his uniform from the Spanish-American War

PICTURETRIVIA

5 POINTS per actor — **Who** are the actors in this film?

5 POINTS — **What** is the title of this film?

5 POINTS — **When** was this film released?

5 POINTS — **Who** is the director of this film?

BONUSTRIVIA

10 POINTS — What was J.J. Gittes' first name (at least the one he went by)?

10 POINTS — What did Gittes find in the landscaped pond in Evelyn Mulwray's back yard?

10 POINTS — What did Gittes say he did when he was working for the District Attorney?

ABOUT THIS MOVIE

A unique blend of classic film noir style and a modern American sensibility, this film was the last one its French-born, Polish director made in the United States. John Huston, who is credited with one of the earliest —if not the first—great films of the noir genre ("The Maltese Falcon"), plays the villain in this film.

Answers • Who? Jack Nicholson **What?** Chinatown **When?** 1974 **Who?** Roman Polanski
Trivia answer 1 Jake
Trivia answer 2 Her husband Hollis' broken eyeglasses
Trivia answer 3 As little as possible

PICTURE TRIVIA

WHO WHAT WHEN & WHERE

(5) POINTS per actor — **Who** are the actors in this film?

(5) POINTS — **What** is the title of this film?

(5) POINTS — **When** was this film released?

(5) POINTS — **Who** is the director of this film?

BONUS TRIVIA

10 POINTS — What did Queeg keep in his pocket and what did he habitually do with them?

10 POINTS — What food item did Queeg claim was stolen by a member of the crew?

10 POINTS — What function did this ship perform for the Navy?

ABOUT THIS MOVIE

It was difficult to get the Navy's cooperation to make a film about a mutiny in the U.S. fleet, but several changes and concessions eventually resulted in their support and approval for this film. The original script (by the author of the original novel, Herman Wouk) ran to 500 pages and had to be severely cut and rewritten. In the end, studio head Harry Cohn demanded the final cut of the film be not a minute longer than two hours and cost not a dollar more than $2 million.

Answers • **Who?** Fred MacMurray, Humphrey Bogart, Robert Francis **What?** The Caine Mutiny **When?** 1954 **Who?** Edward Dmytryk
Trivia answer 1 Steel balls which he constantly rolled in his hand
Trivia answer 2 Frozen strawberries
Trivia answer 3 A mine sweeper

PICTURE TRIVIA

WHO WHAT WHEN & WHERE

5 POINTS per actor — **Who** are the actors in this film?

5 POINTS — **What** is the title of this film?

5 POINTS — **When** was this film released?

5 POINTS — **Who** is the director of this film?

BONUS TRIVIA

10 POINTS — What were Winger's and Zisky's jobs before they enlisted in the army?

10 POINTS — Which Soviet-bloc country did they sneak into to rescue their own unit?

10 POINTS — What was the name of the experimental vehicle being tested in Italy?

ABOUT THIS MOVIE

Filmed largely at the army base in Fort Knox, Kentucky, the stars of this service comedy follow in a long tradition of comics playing characters enlisting in the armed forces, from Abbott and Costello in "Buck Privates" to Pauly Shore in "In the Army Now." The story was originally developed for Cheech and Chong, but their roles were eventually filled by the same pair of actor-comedians who would famously team up again for "Ghostbusters."

Answers • Who? P.J. Soles, Bill Murray **What?** Stripes **When?** 1981 **Who?** Ivan Reitman
Trivia answer 1 Winger drove a taxi and Zisky taught English as a second language
Trivia answer 2 Czechoslovakia
Trivia answer 3 The EM-50 Urban Assault Vehicle

PICTURE TRIVIA

WHO WHAT WHEN & WHERE

⑤ **Who** are the actors in this film?
POINTS per actor

⑤ **What** is the title of this film?
POINTS

⑤ **When** was this film released?
POINTS

⑤ **Who** is the director of this film?
POINTS

BONUS TRIVIA

10 Where was the Navy
POINTS flying school located?

10 Whose dog tags did
POINTS Maverick throw into the
sea after the successful
mission in the Indian
Ocean?

10 What happened to
POINTS Maverick's father in
Vietnam?

ABOUT THIS MOVIE

Like many films featuring one or more arms of the U.S. military, this one got full (Navy) cooperation and support. But since the story took place in a generally peaceful time in America's international affairs, a suitable enemy encounter was somewhat difficult to come by to end the film. A skirmish with aggressive Soviet MIGs over the Indian Ocean was concocted to "test" the training of the fighter pilots.

Answers • Who? Rick Rossovich, Val Kilmer, Anthony Edwards, Tom Cruise **What?** Top Gun **When?** 1986 **Who?** Tony Scott
Trivia answer 1 Miramar, California (in San Diego)
Trivia answer 2 Those of his former copilot, "Goose," who was killed when they had to eject from their plane
Trivia answer 3 He disappeared while flying an F4 on November 5th, 1965

PICTURE TRIVIA

WHO WHAT WHEN & WHERE

(5) POINTS per actor — **Who** are the actors in this film?

(5) POINTS — **What** is the title of this film?

(5) POINTS — **When** was this film released?

(5) POINTS — **Who** is the director of this film?

BONUS TRIVIA

10 POINTS — Who did the girl on the dance floor think she was kissing when she kissed Tony?

10 POINTS — What did Tony's brother do that so disappointed their parents?

10 POINTS — What was the prize amount for the dance contest that Tony and Stephanie won?

ABOUT THIS MOVIE

One of the defining films of the disco era (replete with its ascendance of polyester clothes), this story of living— and dancing —in Brooklyn was a tremendous commercial hit, propelling the now-famous soundtrack into becoming the best-selling album in history for a period of six years.

Answers • Who? John Travolta **What?** Saturday Night Fever **When?** 1977 **Who?** John Badham

Trivia answer 1 Al Pacino
Trivia answer 2 Quit the priesthood
Trivia answer 3 $500

PICTURE TRIVIA

WHO WHAT WHEN & WHERE

⑤ **Who** are the actors in this film?
POINTS per actor

⑤ **What** is the title of this film?
POINTS

⑤ **When** was this film released?
POINTS

⑤ **Who** is the director of this film?
POINTS

BONUS TRIVIA

10 Which airline never
POINTS suffered a crash, according
to Raymond?

10 What TV show did
POINTS Raymond refuse to miss?

10 By Raymond's visual
POINTS count, how many toothpicks
spilled out of the box of
250 in the diner?

ABOUT THIS MOVIE

The inspiration for the character of Raymond in this film is actually based on an amalgamation of several autistic savants, each different from the other. One, for example, could memorize entire phone books, while another could immediately and perfectly play back any piece of music he had just heard.

Answers • Who? Dustin Hoffman, Tom Cruise **What?** Rain Man **When?** 1988 **Who?** Barry Levinson
Trivia answer 1 Qantas
Trivia answer 2 "The People's Court" with Judge Wapner
Trivia answer 3 246 (There were four left in the box)

PICTURE TRIVIA

5 POINTS per actor — **Who** are the actors in this film?

5 POINTS — **What** is the title of this film?

5 POINTS — **When** was this film released?

5 POINTS — **Who** is the director of this film?

BONUS TRIVIA

10 POINTS — Which arm of Helen Kimble's killer was prosthetic?

10 POINTS — What did the son of the landlady (in whose basement Kimble hid) turn out to be?

10 POINTS — At which Chicago hospital did Kimble find the medical records for the one-armed man?

ABOUT THIS MOVIE

Despite the popularity of the original television series and the notoriety of the true story on which the film was loosely based, this feature production concerning Dr. Richard Kimble and his pursuit of the mysterious one-armed man still went through several screenwriters and numerous drafts and changes. The script was constantly revised even during production, and the chase through the St. Patrick's Day parade was filmed ad hoc and unplanned during the actual parade in Chicago.

Answers • Who? Harrison Ford **What?** The Fugitive **When?** 1993 **Who?** Andrew Davis
Trivia answer 1 The right arm
Trivia answer 2 A drug dealer
Trivia answer 3 Cook County Hospital

PICTURETRIVIA

WHO WHAT WHEN & WHERE

(5) **Who** are the actors in this film?
POINTS per actor

(5) **What** is the title of this film?
POINTS

(5) **When** was this film released?
POINTS

(5) **Who** is the director of this film?
POINTS

BONUSTRIVIA

10 What was the one word
POINTS Mr. McGuire had for Ben?

10 What was Mrs. Robinson's
POINTS major in college?

10 What was the name of
POINTS the hotel where Ben and
Mrs. Robinson met?

ABOUT THIS MOVIE

A singularly distinctive film in many ways, it is perhaps the definitive film of the late Sixties. Though the characters and the actors who played them are so iconically familiar to audiences now, Robert Redford, Charles Grodin, and Burt Ward (Robin of the "Batman" TV series fame) were all originally considered for the part of Ben Braddock, and both Doris Day and Patricia Neal were offered the part of Mrs. Robinson.

Answers • Who? Dustin Hoffman, Anne Bancroft **What?** The Graduate **When?** 1967 **Who?** Mike Nichols
Trivia answer 1 Plastics
Trivia answer 2 Art
Trivia answer 3 The Taft Hotel

PICTURE TRIVIA

WHO WHAT WHEN & WHERE

(5 POINTS per actor) **Who** are the actors in this film?

(5 POINTS) **What** is the title of this film?

(5 POINTS) **When** was this film released?

(5 POINTS) **Who** is the director of this film?

BONUS TRIVIA

(10 POINTS) What two types of people did Professor Groeteschele believe would survive a nuclear war?

(10 POINTS) Who was the last person who tried to convince Colonel Grady that the mission was a mistake and the plane should be turned back?

(10 POINTS) On which city did the American jet fighter drop its bomb?

ABOUT THIS MOVIE

This straight dramatic version of a doomsday scenario during the Cold War was somewhat undermined by coming out only eight months after the more farcical treatment of the same plot in "Dr. Strangelove," but its intensity and realism have only improved with age. Ironically, the screenwriter, Walter Bernstein, was blacklisted during the Communist witch hunt era and could not find work for years thereafter. His script stands as a model of compassion, insight, and humanity during a particularly bleak time in recent history.

Answers • Who? Larry Hagman, Henry Fonda **What?** Fail-Safe **When?** 1964 **Who?** Sidney Lumet
Trivia answer 1 Convicts and file clerks
Trivia answer 2 His wife, Helen
Trivia answer 3 Moscow

PICTURE TRIVIA

WHO WHAT WHEN & WHERE

5 POINTS per actor — **Who** are the actors in this film?

5 POINTS — **What** is the title of this film?

5 POINTS — **When** was this film released?

5 POINTS — **Who** is the director of this film?

BONUS TRIVIA

10 POINTS — How many kilos of hashish was Billy caught carrying?

10 POINTS — What was the initial sentence handed down to Billy in the Turkish court?

10 POINTS — Why was getting out on bail the best bet to avoid prison altogether?

ABOUT THIS MOVIE

Based on the true story of Billy Hayes' incarceration in (and escape from) a Turkish prison for attempting to smuggle hashish out of the country, this film recreated Hayes' five-year ordeal with grim realism. Both Richard Gere and John Travolta were initially considered for the role.

Answers • Who? Mike Kellin, Brad Davis **What?** Midnight Express **When?** 1988 **Who?** Alan Parker
Trivia answer 1 Two
Trivia answer 2 Four years, two months
Trivia answer 3 While out on bail, it would be easy to cross the border into Greece and not come back

PICTURE TRIVIA

5 POINTS per actor — **Who** are the actors in this film?

5 POINTS — **What** is the title of this film?

5 POINTS — **When** was this film released?

5 POINTS — **Who** is the director of this film?

BONUS TRIVIA

10 POINTS — Who was John Connor's father?

10 POINTS — How many listings for "Sarah Connor" were in the phone book?

10 POINTS — What make and model number was the first cyborg?

ABOUT THIS MOVIE

This low budget, little heralded science fiction thriller launched the careers of the director and its leading actor, spawned a bigger and even more successful sequel, and provided a signature catchphrase ("I'll be back") for its star for the rest of his career.

Answers • Who? Arnold Schwarzenegger **What?** The Terminator **When?** 1984 **Who?** James Cameron
Trivia answer 1 Kyle Reese
Trivia answer 2 Three
Trivia answer 3 Cyberdyne Systems Model 101

PICTURE TRIVIA

WHO WHAT WHEN & WHERE

5 POINTS per actor — **Who** are the actors in this film?

5 POINTS — **What** is the title of this film?

5 POINTS — **When** was this film released?

5 POINTS — **Who** is the director of this film?

BONUS TRIVIA

10 POINTS — What was John Robie known as at the height of his thieving days?

10 POINTS — What did Robie do during the war?

10 POINTS — At what famous hotel on the Riviera did Robie meet the Stevens?

ABOUT THIS MOVIE

The third of four films made by this star and director team brought the star, who was flirting with quitting acting altogether at the time, out of his semi-retirement. They went on to make a fourth film together, "North By Northwest," in 1959. The star then continued working until his actual retirement in 1966.

Answers • **Who?** Cary Grant, Grace Kelly **What?** To Catch a Thief **When?** 1955 **Who?** Alfred Hitchcock
Trivia answer 1 "The Cat"
Trivia answer 2 Fought with the French Resistance
Trivia answer 3 The Hotel Carlton

PICTURE TRIVIA

WHO WHAT WHEN & WHERE

5 POINTS per actor — **Who** are the actors in this film?

5 POINTS — **What** is the title of this film?

5 POINTS — **When** was this film released?

5 POINTS — **Who** is the director of this film?

BONUS TRIVIA

10 POINTS — What was the "demon that lived in the air"?

10 POINTS — How many astronauts were initially selected for the Mercury program?

10 POINTS — What two additions to the Mercury capsule did the astronauts demand be included?

ABOUT THIS MOVIE

As much a tale of the early test pilots and the first Mercury astronauts as it was a study of America's fascination with celebrity and hero worship, the director's adaptation of Tom Wolfe's best-selling novel neither ignited at the box office nor helped the real John Glenn's presidential ambitions at the time of the film's release.

Answers • Who? Fred Ward, Dennis Quaid, Scott Paulin, Ed Harris, Charles Frank, Scott Glenn, Lance Henriksen **What?** The Right Stuff **When?** 1983 **Who?** Philip Kaufman
Trivia answer 1 The sound barrier
Trivia answer 2 Seven
Trivia answer 3 Explosive bolts for the hatch and a window

PICTURE TRIVIA

WHO WHAT WHEN & WHERE

5 POINTS per actor — **Who** are the actors in this film?

5 POINTS — **What** is the title of this film?

5 POINTS — **When** was this film released?

5 POINTS — **Who** is the director of this film?

BONUS TRIVIA

10 POINTS — What was the name of the featured TV show?

10 POINTS — Which New York borough was Herbie Stempel from?

10 POINTS — What was the question that Van Doren deliberately got wrong?

ABOUT THIS MOVIE

The real Charles Van Doren refused to cooperate in the making of this film. The real Herbie Stempel, whom Van Doren beat by cheating, endorsed the film but didn't think the actor who played him did an accurate impersonation. "I don't think I'm that hyper," Stempel said in a TV interview. Watch for the cameo roles of two well known film directors: Martin Scorsese and Barry Levinson.

Answers • Who? Ralph Fiennes **What?** Quiz Show **When?** 1994 **Who?** Robert Redford
Trivia answer 1 "Twenty One"
Trivia answer 2 Queens
Trivia answer 3 Who was the King of Belgium? (He answered the other three parts correctly, naming the kings of Norway, Sweden, and Iraq)

PICTURE TRIVIA

WHO WHAT WHEN & WHERE

5 POINTS per actor
Who are the actors in this film?

5 POINTS
What is the title of this film?

5 POINTS
When was this film released?

5 POINTS
Who is the director of this film?

BONUS TRIVIA

10 POINTS
What was the name of the political candidate Travis Bickle stalked?

10 POINTS
What was the name of the dirty movie Travis took Betsy to see on their date?

10 POINTS
How old was Iris, according to what Sport told Travis?

ABOUT THIS MOVIE

Almost a genre in itself (described by the director as "New York Gothic"), this film remains a potent tale of a society at its lowest point, with an extremely unlikely knight saving an equally unlikely damsel in distress. The famous "You talking to me?" mirror soliloquy is known by more people today than have even seen the film.

Answers • **Who?** Jodie Foster, Robert De Niro **What?** Taxi Driver **When?** 1976 **Who?** Martin Scorsese
Trivia answer 1 Charles Palantine
Trivia answer 2 "Sometime Sweet Susan"
Trivia answer 3 12 1/2

PICTURE TRIVIA

WHO WHAT WHEN & WHERE

5 POINTS per actor **Who** are the actors in this film?

5 POINTS **What** is the title of this film?

5 POINTS **When** was this film released?

5 POINTS **Who** is the director of this film?

BONUS TRIVIA

10 POINTS What did Beth find boiling in the pot when the Gallaghers returned home from visiting the grandparents?

10 POINTS What opera did both Dan and Alex consider their favorite?

10 POINTS What was the name of the "exercise manual" being promoted at the book signing where Dan first met Alex?

ABOUT THIS MOVIE

The original ending for this film, with the victimized husband being arrested and led away by police, was apparently too depressing to preview audiences, so the cast and crew reassembled to shoot a different ending. Apparently that did the trick, as the film became a big commercial hit.

Answers • Who? Glenn Close, Michael Douglas, Ann Archer **What?** Fatal Attraction **When?** 1987 **Who?** Adrian Lyne
Trivia answer 1 Whitly, the pet rabbit
Trivia answer 2 "Madame Butterfly"
Trivia answer 3 "Samurai Self-Help"

PICTURE TRIVIA

WHO WHAT WHEN & WHERE

5 POINTS per actor — **Who** are the actors in this film?

5 POINTS — **What** is the title of this film?

5 POINTS — **When** was this film released?

5 POINTS — **Who** is the director of this film?

BONUS TRIVIA

10 POINTS — What song was Reggie belting out in his prison cell when Jack went to meet him?

10 POINTS — What does the title of the film refer to?

10 POINTS — Where did Reggie hide the half million dollars?

ABOUT THIS MOVIE

The star was only 21 years old in this movie, his feature film debut. Though he and his costar got along well and created great bickering chemistry as the leads, he had to work hard to persuade his former partner to make the sequel eight years later.

Answers • Who? Nick Nolte, Eddie Murphy **What?** 48 Hours **When?** 1982 **Who?** Walter Hill
Trivia answer 1 "Roxanne" by the Police
Trivia answer 2 The amount of time Reggie was allowed out of prison in Jack's custody
Trivia answer 3 In the trunk of his car

PICTURE TRIVIA

5 POINTS per actor — **Who** are the actors in this film?

5 POINTS — **What** is the title of this film?

5 POINTS — **When** was this film released?

5 POINTS — **Who** is the director of this film?

BONUS TRIVIA

10 POINTS — What football position did Joe Pendleton play and for what team?

10 POINTS — What musical instrument did Joe like to play?

10 POINTS — What was the name of the English town threatened to be displaced by one of Farnsworth's enterprises?

ABOUT THIS MOVIE

This film featured the third teaming of the male and female stars (the first two being "McCabe and Mrs. Miller" and "Shampoo"). An updated remake of 1941's "Here Comes Mr. Jordan," this version changes Joe's original sport of boxing, but keeps Mr. Jordan essentially — and mysteriously — British.

Answers • Who? Dick Enberg, Warren Beatty **What?** Heaven Can Wait **When?** 1978 **Who?** Warren Beatty and Buck Henry
Trivia answer 1 Quarterback for the Los Angeles Rams
Trivia answer 2 Soprano saxophone
Trivia answer 3 Pagglesham

PICTURE TRIVIA

WHO WHAT WHEN & WHERE

5 POINTS per actor — **Who** are the actors in this film?

5 POINTS — **What** is the title of this film?

5 POINTS — **When** was this film released?

5 POINTS — **Who** is the director of this film?

BONUS TRIVIA

10 POINTS — What was John Prentiss' profession and specialty?

10 POINTS — Where were John and Joanna flying in from before meeting Joanna's parents?

10 POINTS — What was the age difference between John and Joanna?

This was a movie of firsts and lasts: the first film with a positive story and a happy ending for an interracial relationship, and the last film with the veteran actor who played the father, who died just ten days after finishing his part. It was also the ninth and last film the two "parents" made together.

Answers • Who? Sidney Poitier, Katharine Houghton, Katharine Hepburn, Spencer Tracy **What?** Guess Who's Coming to Dinner **When?** 1967
Who? Stanley Kramer
Trivia answer 1 He was a doctor working for the World Health Organization in Geneva, specializing in tropical diseases
Trivia answer 2 Hawaii
Trivia answer 3 14 years; he was 37 and she was 23

144

PICTURE TRIVIA

5 POINTS per actor — **Who** are the actors in this film?

5 POINTS — **What** is the title of this film?

5 POINTS — **When** was this film released?

5 POINTS — **Who** is the director of this film?

BONUS TRIVIA

10 POINTS — What did Szell hope to retrieve from a safe deposit box in New York City?

10 POINTS — What was Doc's secret name working for The Division?

10 POINTS — What country did Opal claim she was from before Doc discovered that she was lying?

ABOUT THIS MOVIE

The star in this film was concerned that he might be too old (he was 38 when filming began) to be playing a graduate student in his mid-twenties. The aging veteran actor who played the villain Szell was suffering from one of several bouts he endured with cancer at the time, and it was difficult some days for him to even walk. The filmmakers hid his illness as best they could, and no one who didn't already know about his health could tell from watching him in the movie.

Answers • Who? Roy Scheider, Dustin Hoffman **What?** Marathon Man **When?** 1976 **Who?** John Schlesinger
Trivia answer 1 Diamonds
Trivia answer 2 Scylla
Trivia answer 3 Switzerland

PICTURE TRIVIA

WHO WHAT WHEN & WHERE

5 POINTS per actor — **Who** are the actors in this film?

5 POINTS — **What** is the title of this film?

5 POINTS — **When** was this film released?

5 POINTS — **Who** is the director of this film?

BONUS TRIVIA

10 POINTS — What did they call the shed in which Nicholson was thrown for punishment?

10 POINTS — How long did Colonel Nicholson expect the bridge to endure?

10 POINTS — What two cities would be linked together by rail via completion of the bridge?

ABOUT THIS MOVIE

The first of the director's "epic masterpieces" (the other two being "Lawrence of Arabia" and "Doctor Zhivago"), this film transformed the British film industry from a producer of smaller comedies and dramas about colorful, eccentric characters and subjects into Hollywood's equivalent for spectacle and action, at least for the following decade.

Answers • Who? Jack Hawkins, Sir Alec Guinness **What?** The Bridge on the River Kwai **When?** 1957 **Who?** David Lean
Trivia answer 1 The Oven
Trivia answer 2 600 years
Trivia answer 3 Bangkok and Rangoon

PICTURE TRIVIA

WHO WHAT WHEN & WHERE

(5) POINTS per actor **Who** are the actors in this film?

(5) POINTS **What** is the title of this film?

(5) POINTS **When** was this film released?

(5) POINTS **Who** is the director of this film?

BONUS TRIVIA

10 POINTS What was Dexter Haven's nickname for Traci?

10 POINTS What was the name of the boat Dexter Haven designed and built, which he and Traci sailed along the coast of Maine for their honeymoon?

10 POINTS What was the name of the magazine Macauley Connor worked for?

ABOUT THIS MOVIE

The success story of this film is the leading lady's personal success story as well. After starring in the stage version, she bought the rights and handpicked the director, screenwriter, and cast. Following several commercial flops, and having been labeled "box office poison," she came back with this film, which made a record $100,000 average take a week after opening at Radio City Music Hall.

Answers • Who? Cary Grant, Katharine Hepburn, James Stewart, Ruth Hussey **What?** The Philadelphia Story **When?** 1940 **Who?** George Cukor

Trivia answer 1 Red
Trivia answer 2 True Love
Trivia answer 3 "Spy" magazine

PICTURETRIVIA

WHO WHAT WHEN & WHERE

5 POINTS per actor — **Who** are the actors in this film?

5 POINTS — **What** is the title of this film?

5 POINTS — **When** was this film released?

5 POINTS — **Who** is the director of this film?

BONUSTRIVIA

10 POINTS — Through what part of her body did Sarah claim to be able to feel the vibrations of music on a dance floor?

10 POINTS — What were the reasons Sarah gave for liking her cleaning job at the school?

10 POINTS — What items were on the list, taped to the mirror, that Sarah was memorizing?

ABOUT THIS MOVIE

The lead actress won a Best Actress Oscar for her performance in this film, her feature film debut. Since she is deaf in real life and was portrayed to be deaf in the film, in order to give her lines of dialogue, the lead actor repeated aloud what she "said" in sign language as they conversed. This technique worked so well it has now become a common way of performing scenes with a deaf character.

Answers • Who? William Hurt, Marlee Matlin **What?** Children of a Lesser God **When?** 1986 **Who?** Randa Haines
Trivia answer 1 Her nose
Trivia answer 2 It was a job she could do alone, and in silence
Trivia answer 3 The different hands of poker, for an evening of playing at the Franklins

PICTURE TRIVIA

5 POINTS per actor — **Who** are the actors in this film?

5 POINTS — **What** is the title of this film?

5 POINTS — **When** was this film released?

5 POINTS — **Who** is the director of this film?

BONUS TRIVIA

10 POINTS — What did Mitch and his friends do the year before going to the cattle ranch?

10 POINTS — What made the cattle stampede?

10 POINTS — What did Mitch name the calf he helped birth?

Upon accepting a Best Supporting Actor Oscar for portraying the hard-bitten, taciturn cattle-drive master in this film, the legendary but aging actor who played Curly reaffirmed his physical prowess by doing one-armed pushups in front of the live Oscar audience — and a good percentage of the rest of the world watching on TV.

Answers • Who? Daniel Stern, David Paymer, Helen Slater, Josh Mostel, Billy Crystal, Bruno Kirby **What?** City Slickers **When?** 1991 **Who?** Ron Underwood
Trivia answer 1 Ran with the bulls at Pamplona, Spain
Trivia answer 2 The noise from Mitch's coffee grinder
Trivia answer 3 Norman

PICTURE TRIVIA

WHO WHAT WHEN & WHERE

5 POINTS per actor — **Who** are the actors in this film?

5 POINTS — **What** is the title of this film?

5 POINTS — **When** was this film released?

5 POINTS — **Who** is the director of this film?

BONUS TRIVIA

10 POINTS — Why was this one of the last opportunities to ride this particular river?

10 POINTS — What did the banjo boy do when Drew offered to shake his hand?

10 POINTS — What kind of weapon did Lewis use to kill their attackers?

ABOUT THIS MOVIE

The actor who played Lewis regarded his role in this movie as one of the highlights of his career. He got the role after Marlon Brando, James Stewart, and Henry Fonda all turned it down — due, it is said, to the obvious hazards they would have had to confront on location, riding the treacherous river seen in the film. Having been a stunt man before becoming an actor, this actor performed all his own stunts in the movie, including going over a waterfall and riding the rapids.

Answers • Who? Burt Reynolds, Ned Beatty **What?** Deliverance **When?** 1972 **Who?** John Boorman
Trivia answer 1 A dam would soon be built that would flood the area completely
Trivia answer 2 Turned his head to the side and ignored him
Trivia answer 3 A bow and arrow

PICTURE TRIVIA

WHO WHAT WHEN & WHERE

5 POINTS per actor — **Who** are the actors in this film?

5 POINTS — **What** is the title of this film?

5 POINTS — **When** was this film released?

5 POINTS — **Who** is the director of this film?

BONUS TRIVIA

10 POINTS — What did Joe Buck do for a living before deciding to become a hustler?

10 POINTS — What was Ratzo's real name?

10 POINTS — Where did Ratzo want to go when he finally left New York City?

ABOUT THIS MOVIE

After his breakout role in "The Graduate," the star of this film took on the challenge of becoming Ratzo Rizzo, a character as far away from Benjamin Braddock as he could get. To convince the producer of his capability of playing the seedy Rizzo, he dressed in character and pretended to be a real bum at the place where they were scheduled to meet.

Answers • Who? Jon Voight, Dustin Hoffman **What?** Midnight Cowboy **When?** 1969 **Who?** John Schlesinger
Trivia answer 1 He worked as a dishwasher
Trivia answer 2 Enrico Salvatore Rizzo
Trivia answer 3 Florida

PICTURE TRIVIA

WHO WHAT WHEN & WHERE

(5) POINTS per actor — **Who** are the actors in this film?

(5) POINTS — **What** is the title of this film?

(5) POINTS — **When** was this film released?

(5) POINTS — **Who** is the director of this film?

BONUS TRIVIA

10 POINTS — How did Ronny Cammareri lose his hand?

10 POINTS — How was Loretta's first husband killed?

10 POINTS — Which opera did Ronny take Loretta to at the Met?

Answers • Who? Olympia Dukakis, Cher **What?** Moonstruck **When?** 1987 **Who?** Norman Jewison
Trivia answer 1 It was caught in a bread slicer
Trivia answer 2 He was hit by a bus
Trivia answer 3 "La Bohème"

PICTURE TRIVIA

WHO WHAT WHEN & WHERE

5 POINTS per actor — **Who** are the actors in this film?

5 POINTS — **What** is the title of this film?

5 POINTS — **When** was this film released?

5 POINTS — **Who** is the director of this film?

BONUS TRIVIA

10 POINTS — What items did Ensign Pulver want to put in the captain's overhead bin?

10 POINTS — What was the name of the cargo ship the executive officer and crew were on?

10 POINTS — What did the crew name the homemade medal they gave as a farewell gift?

ABOUT THIS MOVIE

Based on the Broadway play of the same name, this film was considered by its star to be his favorite role. The film featured a mixed ensemble of veteran stars, including William Powell in his last film role as the ship's doctor, and newcomers, most notably the up-and-coming young actor who played Ensign Pulver, Jack Lemmon.

Answers • Who? James Cagney, Henry Fonda **What?** Mister Roberts **When?** 1955 **Who?** John Ford, Mervyn LeRoy, Joshua Logan
Trivia answer 1 Marbles, so that they would roll around all night and keep him awake
Trivia answer 2 The Reluctant
Trivia answer 3 The Order of the Palm

PICTURE TRIVIA

⑤ **Who** are the actors in this film?
POINTS per actor

⑤ **What** is the title of this film?
POINTS

⑤ **When** was this film released?
POINTS

⑤ **Who** is the director of this film?
POINTS

BONUS TRIVIA

10 In what city and country did the story take place?
POINTS

10 What was the black powdery substance found in the wine bottles?
POINTS

10 What was Alicia Huberman's father convicted of?
POINTS

ABOUT THIS MOVIE

One of its director's best, this film contains nearly all his signature touches: a MacGuffin, a domineering mother figure, a suave and cultured villain, exotic locales, a director's cameo, and plenty of suspenseful twists and turns. Made just at the end of World War II, it was prescient in presenting a story involving ex-Nazis escaped to South America and research into using uranium isotopes to develop an atomic bomb.

Answers • Who? Cary Grant, Ingrid Bergman **What?** Notorious **When?** 1946 **Who?** Alfred Hitchcock
Trivia answer 1 Rio, Brazil
Trivia answer 2 Sand containing uranium ore
Trivia answer 3 Treason against the United States

PICTURE TRIVIA

5 POINTS per actor — **Who** are the actors in this film?

5 POINTS — **What** is the title of this film?

5 POINTS — **When** was this film released?

5 POINTS — **Who** is the director of this film?

BONUS TRIVIA

10 POINTS — What were the penalties for attempted escapes by a convict?

10 POINTS — What was Louis Dega's criminal expertise?

10 POINTS — While studying the tides, which number wave in the series did Henri calculate was big enough to carry him out to sea and beyond the point of return?

ABOUT THIS MOVIE

With one classic escape film ("The Great Escape") already behind him, the star of this film took on the role of the only man to escape from Devil's Island. At the time of its release, the realism of the film (which included an onscreen execution by guillotine) was remarkable. The costar who played Dega even used contact lenses so as to be able to see clearly through the real (and really thick) eyeglasses his character had to wear throughout the film.

Answers • Who? Steve McQueen, Dustin Hoffman **What?** Papillon **When?** 1973 **Who?** Franklin J. Schaffner
Trivia answer 1 For the first attempt, add two years in solitary on top of existing sentence; for the second attempt, an additional five years
Trivia answer 2 He was a counterfeiter
Trivia answer 3 The seventh

PICTURE TRIVIA

WHO WHAT WHEN & WHERE

5 POINTS per actor — **Who** are the actors in this film?

5 POINTS — **What** is the title of this film?

5 POINTS — **When** was this film released?

5 POINTS — **Who** is the director of this film?

BONUS TRIVIA

10 POINTS — What did Esther feel compelled to do every time something happened to her, good or bad?

10 POINTS — What movie starring Norman Maine was playing in the theater before the sneak preview of Vicki's film?

10 POINTS — What was Norman Maine's real "birth" name?

ABOUT THIS MOVIE

The star's real birth name, Frances Ethel Gumm, was remarkably similar to that of Esther Blodgett, the main character who became Vicki Lester in this film. Many events in the movie paralleled her turbulent personal life at the time, and many reviewers commented on how realistic her performance was. As a final irony, the actor who played her doomed husband in the film gave the eulogy at her funeral in New York in 1969.

Answers • Who? James Mason, Judy Garland **What?** A Star is Born **When?** 1954 **Who?** George Cukor

Trivia answer 1 Wash her hair

Trivia answer 2 "Another Dawn"

Trivia answer 3 Ernest Sidney Gubbins

PICTURETRIVIA

WHO WHAT WHEN & WHERE

(5) POINTS per actor — **Who** are the actors in this film?

(5) POINTS — **What** is the title of this film?

(5) POINTS — **When** was this film released?

(5) POINTS — **Who** is the director of this film?

BONUSTRIVIA

10 POINTS — What music was played during the helicopter attack on the village?

10 POINTS — What did Colonel Kilgore think napalm in the morning smelled like?

10 POINTS — Which major star played the one-scene cameo role of a certain "Colonel G. Lucas"?

ABOUT THIS MOVIE

This film, made under chaotic and oppressive conditions that nearly drove the director to a nervous breakdown and its original star to a heart attack, ultimately became one of the most provocative and controversial films in movie history. It has the dubious distinction of exposing the most celluloid ever for a movie (over 1,250,000 feet). Despite the travails of its production, it went on to win the biggest prize at Cannes and initiated a period of Vietnam war films that included "Platoon" and "Full Metal Jacket."

Answers • Who? Dennis Hopper, Martin Sheen **What?** Apocalypse Now **When?** 1979 **Who?** Francis Ford Coppola
Trivia answer 1 Wagner's "Ride Of The Valkyries"
Trivia answer 2 Victory
Trivia answer 3 Harrison Ford

PICTURE TRIVIA

WHO WHAT WHEN & WHERE

5 POINTS per actor **Who** are the actors in this film?

5 POINTS **What** is the title of this film?

5 POINTS **When** was this film released?

5 POINTS **Who** is the director of this film?

BONUS TRIVIA

10 POINTS In what year does the story take place?

10 POINTS What was the name of the corporation that built replicants?

10 POINTS Which series number of the "Nexus" replicants have returned to Earth?

ABOUT THIS MOVIE

In this film, the distinctive look of a future Los Angeles was developed in great part by Syd Mead, a former industrial designer working at Ford Motor Company. His signature contribution was the "Spinners," the airborne police vehicles seen in the film.

Answers • Who? Harrison Ford **What?** Blade Runner **When?** 1982 **Who?** Ridley Scott
Trivia answer 1 2019
Trivia answer 2 The Tyrell Corporation
Trivia answer 3 The Nexus 6 Series

PICTURE TRIVIA

5 POINTS per actor · **Who** are the actors in this film?

5 POINTS · **What** is the title of this film?

5 POINTS · **When** was this film released?

5 POINTS · **Who** is the director of this film?

BONUS TRIVIA

10 POINTS · What was Saunders' sarcastic nickname for Jefferson?

10 POINTS · What famous Senator's desk did Jefferson inherit?

10 POINTS · What was the purpose of the bill he introduced in the Senate?

ABOUT THIS MOVIE

Now regarded as one of several classic films from the banner movie year of 1939, this film got the opposite reaction when it opened, eliciting heavy criticism for its portrayal of the inner workings of American politics. The scene between Jefferson Smith and Clarissa Saunders, in which Saunders describes the delays, manipulations, and revisions that will inevitably take over the bill Smith intends to introduce, is a classic—and a relevant lesson in how government works today.

Answers • Who? James Stewart **What?** Mr. Smith Goes to Washington **When?** 1939 **Who?** Frank Capra
Trivia answer 1 Daniel Boone
Trivia answer 2 Daniel Webster's
Trivia answer 3 The creation of a national boys' camp

PICTURE TRIVIA

5 POINTS per actor — **Who** are the actors in this film?

5 POINTS — **What** is the title of this film?

5 POINTS — **When** was this film released?

5 POINTS — **Who** is the director of this film?

BONUS TRIVIA

10 POINTS — Through what medium did "they" first reach out to Carol Anne?

10 POINTS — What did the real estate developers neglect to do when they moved the cemetery?

10 POINTS — Was it a good thing or not to "go into the light"?

ABOUT THIS MOVIE

This film about a haunting of a suburban California family created a supernatural phenomenon by pulling both the oldest and newest rabbits out of the special effects hat. While exploiting the latest optical effects created by George Lucas' Industrial Light and Magic, some very simple tricks of the trade were also employed, like panning away from a kitchen table by following an actor and then returning to find all the chairs suddenly stacked on top, a trick accomplished with a prepared stack of chairs all glued together.

Answers • Who? Craig T. Nelson, Heather O'Rourke, Jobeth Williams **What?** Poltergeist **When?** 1982 **Who?** Tobe Hooper
Trivia answer 1 The television set
Trivia answer 2 Move the bodies (they only moved the headstones)
Trivia answer 3 Not a good thing

PICTURETRIVIA

⑤ **Who** are the actors in this film?
POINTS per actor

⑤ **What** is the title of this film?
POINTS

⑤ **When** was this film released?
POINTS

⑤ **Who** is the director of this film?
POINTS

BONUSTRIVIA

10 Where did Johnny Hooker
POINTS ply his trade before going to
Chicago?

10 Where did Henry Gondorff
POINTS live and work when Johnny
met up with him in Chicago?

10 How much did Doyle
POINTS Lonnegan bet (and
subsequently lose)
during the final big con?

ABOUT THIS MOVIE

This film was the only other pairing of the two male leads after their hugely popular teaming in "Butch Cassidy and the Sundance Kid" (which also featured the same director). Unlike "Butch," which was filmed on location, nearly all of this film was shot on the studio backlot, dressed to look like Chicago in 1936. A professional card player performed the card tricks that Harry is seen performing, and the villain's limp was the result of a real injury that the actor playing Doyle sustained just before filming began.

Answers • Who? Paul Newman, Robert Redford **What?** The Sting **When?** 1973 **Who?** George Roy Hill
Trivia answer 1 Joliet, Illinois
Trivia answer 2 At a merry-go-round hall, where Henry did the repairs
Trivia answer 3 $500,000

PICTURETRIVIA

WHO WHAT WHEN & WHERE

5 POINTS per actor — **Who** are the actors in this film?

5 POINTS — **What** is the title of this film?

5 POINTS — **When** was this film released?

5 POINTS — **Who** is the director of this film?

BONUSTRIVIA

10 POINTS — What was Crash Davis' first lesson for "Nuke" LaLoosh?

10 POINTS — What do minor leaguers call being in a major league game?

10 POINTS — How did Crash get the team a "rain-out" to give them a much needed night off?

ABOUT THIS MOVIE

Life in the baseball minor leagues hadn't been portrayed with such accuracy and honesty until this film, written and directed by an actual former minor leaguer, came along. The shooting went late into the year, well past baseball season, and problems with trees changing color and the breath of actors condensing during filming added to production woes. To alleviate such problems, many scenes became night games, and the grass on the playing field, which turned brown before shooting concluded, had to be painted green.

Answers • Who? Tim Robbins, Susan Sarandon **What?** Bull Durham **When?** 1988 **Who?** Ron Shelton

Trivia answer 1 Don't think, it can only hurt the ball club

Trivia answer 2 Being "in the show"

Trivia answer 3 By turning on all the sprinklers to flood the ball field they were scheduled to play on

PICTURE TRIVIA

⑤ **Who** are the actors in this film?
POINTS per actor

⑤ **What** is the title of this film?
POINTS

⑤ **When** was this film released?
POINTS

⑤ **Who** is the director of this film?
POINTS

BONUS TRIVIA

10 What was the reason
POINTS for Randall McMurphy's commitment to the mental institution?

10 Who did McMurphy claim he
POINTS and the patients were when going out on the boat trip?

10 What did McMurphy offer
POINTS Chief that made him speak?

ABOUT THIS MOVIE

This was only the second film (the first was 1934's "It Happened One Night") to sweep the Oscars in the major categories, its "Bests" including Picture, Director, Actor, Actress, and Screenplay. Rights to Ken Kesey's novel were bought and held by Kirk Douglas for years while he tried to get the film financed so that he could play McMurphy. Eventually Kirk's son Michael got the ball rolling (as producer) and enlisted the same director his father originally had in mind.

Answers • Who? Danny DeVito, Jack Nicholson, Brad Dourif, William Redfield **What?** One Flew Over the Cuckoo's Nest **When?** 1975 **Who?** Milos Forman
Trivia answer 1 To evaluate whether he was faking insanity in order to get out of his prison work detail
Trivia answer 2 The staff of the state mental institution
Trivia answer 3 A stick of Juicy Fruit gum

PICTURETRIVIA

WHO WHAT WHEN & WHERE

(5) POINTS per actor — **Who** are the actors in this film?

(5) POINTS — **What** is the title of this film?

(5) POINTS — **When** was this film released?

(5) POINTS — **Who** is the director of this film?

BONUSTRIVIA

10 POINTS — In what sea was the island where the commando team was sent?

10 POINTS — How high was the sheer cliff that the team had to scale?

10 POINTS — What kind of explosive was initially in the plan to blow up the guns?

ABOUT THIS MOVIE

This film went through several complete changes of cast and director before shooting began. At one time Alec Guinness, William Holden, and Marlon Brando were cast in the major roles. The final team proved to be a winning one, both critically and at the box office.

Answers • Who? Anthony Quinn, David Niven, Gregory Peck **What?** The Guns of Navarone **When?** 1961 **Who?** J. Lee Thompson
Trivia answer 1 The Aegean
Trivia answer 2 400 feet
Trivia answer 3 Fulminate of mercury

PICTURETRIVIA

WHOWHATWHEN&WHERE

5 POINTS per actor **Who** are the actors in this film?

5 POINTS **What** is the title of this film?

5 POINTS **When** was this film released?

5 POINTS **Who** is the director of this film?

BONUSTRIVIA

10 POINTS How old was John Merrick when Frederick Treves discovered him?

10 POINTS Which limb of John Merrick's was the only one that was perfectly normal?

10 POINTS What did John Merrick recite which revealed he could speak and knew how to read?

Two productions of this story happened contemporaneously: this film and a stage play, and they were unrelated to each other. In the stage play, by Bernard Pomerance, no makeup was used to represent the protagonist's real deformities, while the actor's makeup in the film was based on castings from the actual skeleton of the famous "freak" of English Victorian times who was the focus of the story.

Answers • Who? Anthony Hopkins, John Hurt **What?** The Elephant Man **When?** 1980 **Who?** David Lynch
Trivia answer 1 21
Trivia answer 2 His left arm
Trivia answer 3 The 23rd Psalm from the Bible

PICTURE TRIVIA

WHO WHAT WHEN & WHERE

5 POINTS per actor — **Who** are the actors in this film?

5 POINTS — **What** is the title of this film?

5 POINTS — **When** was this film released?

5 POINTS — **Who** is the director of this film?

BONUS TRIVIA

10 POINTS — What were the names of the two rival gangs?

10 POINTS — Where did Tony and Maria first meet?

10 POINTS — Which gang members were killed in the rumble?

ABOUT THIS MOVIE

This film placed Shakespeare's "Romeo and Juliet" in New York City and turned the Montagues and Capulets into rival street gangs. The original script was about a Protestant boy meeting a Jewish girl on the east side of New York. Both Marlon Brando and Elvis Presley were originally considered for the part of Tony, while Barbara Luna was considered for Maria.

Answers • Who? Richard Beymer, Natalie Wood **What?** West Side Story **When?** 1961 **Who?** Robert Wise
Trivia answer 1 The Sharks and the Jets
Trivia answer 2 At the dance in the gym
Trivia answer 3 Bernardo and Riff

PICTURE TRIVIA

5 POINTS per actor — **Who** are the actors in this film?

5 POINTS — **What** is the title of this film?

5 POINTS — **When** was this film released?

5 POINTS — **Who** is the director of this film?

BONUS TRIVIA

10 POINTS — How did the judge secure an untainted jury for Al Capone's trial?

10 POINTS — What memento of Malone's did Ness bestow to Malone's fellow cop George Stone?

10 POINTS — What was Elliot Ness going to do if Prohibition ended?

ABOUT THIS MOVIE

This film's director is known for his reconstructions of famous scenes from earlier films. In this film, the train station sequence where the baby carriage flies precariously down the steps during the gunfight is based on the Odessa steps sequence in the silent Russian film "Potemkin."

Answers • Who? Sean Connery, Kevin Costner **What?** The Untouchables **When?** 1987 **Who?** Brian De Palma
Trivia answer 1 He switched his jury with that of the jury for the trial going on in the adjacent courtroom
Trivia answer 2 Malone's call box key, chained to a medal of St. Jude, the patron saint of lost causes and policemen
Trivia answer 3 Have a drink

PICTURE TRIVIA

5 POINTS per actor — **Who** are the actors in this film?

5 POINTS — **What** is the title of this film?

5 POINTS — **When** was this film released?

5 POINTS — **Who** is the director of this film?

BONUS TRIVIA

10 POINTS — What does this film's title refer to?

10 POINTS — Near which city was the power plant located?

10 POINTS — What did the power plant inspector do wrong?

ABOUT THIS MOVIE

A mere week into its theatrical release, this film's subject—an accident at a nuclear power plant—really occurred, at the Three Mile Island nuclear facility in Pennsylvania. The film is also notable for not having a musical score anywhere throughout the film, with the exception of a song over the opening credits.

Answers • Who? Michael Douglas, Jane Fonda **What?** The China Syndrome **When?** 1979 **Who?** James Bridges
Trivia answer 1 The script's conjecture that a nuclear accident would generate uncontrollable heat sufficient to melt the floor of the power plant and then continue through the ground, conceivably all the way to China
Trivia answer 2 Los Angeles
Trivia answer 3 Signed off repeatedly on the same X-rays of welds instead of getting new X-rays

PICTURETRIVIA

⑤ **Who** are the actors in this film?
POINTS per actor

⑤ **What** is the title of this film?
POINTS

⑤ **When** was this film released?
POINTS

⑤ **Who** is the director of this film?
POINTS

BONUSTRIVIA

10 What was Jake LaMotta's
POINTS weight class?

10 How old was Vickie when
POINTS Jake first set eyes on her at
the municipal pool?

10 Who was Jake's opponent
POINTS in the match where he
deliberately threw the fight?

The fight scenes in this movie are duly celebrated for the innovative techniques used to shoot them. Slow motion, variable speed, 360 degree pans, and tilted camera angles were all fused together to portray each fight differently. The goal was to recreate the style and spirit of the tabloid photography of the time, with its harsh lighting, stark expressions, and feel of a brutally violent experience.

Answers • Who? Cathy Moriarty, Robert De Niro **What?** Raging Bull **When?** 1980 **Who?** Martin Scorsese
Trivia answer 1 Middleweight
Trivia answer 2 15
Trivia answer 3 Middleweight champion Billy Fox

PICTURE TRIVIA

WHO WHAT WHEN & WHERE

5 POINTS per actor — **Who** are the actors in this film?

5 POINTS — **What** is the title of this film?

5 POINTS — **When** was this film released?

5 POINTS — **Who** is the director of this film?

BONUS TRIVIA

10 POINTS — How many horses did Judah drive in the chariot race?

10 POINTS — To what did Messala and Judah toast upon their initial reunion?

10 POINTS — What were the three Roman galley rowing speeds that led up to ramming speed?

ABOUT THIS MOVIE

Sharing the record for the most Oscars (11, along with "Titanic" and "The Return of The King"), this film likely missed getting an unprecedented twelfth Oscar for Best Screenplay due to a public and protracted dispute over screenwriting credits. The studio, MGM, was saved from near-bankruptcy by the success of this film, which featured arguably the subtlest depiction ever of Christ (never seen on screen and depicted solely by the reactions of characters who do see Him).

Answers • Who? Charlton Heston **What?** Ben-Hur **When?** 1959 **Who?** William Wyler
Trivia answer 1 Four
Trivia answer 2 The loyalty of old friends
Trivia answer 3 Normal, Battle, and Attack

PICTURE TRIVIA

5 POINTS per actor — **Who** are the actors in this film?

5 POINTS — **What** is the title of this film?

5 POINTS — **When** was this film released?

5 POINTS — **Who** is the director of this film?

BONUS TRIVIA

10 POINTS — What did all the friends do for a living in their hometown?

10 POINTS — What detail (seen by the audience but not by the characters) presaged bad luck at the wedding?

10 POINTS — How many bullets did Michael trick his captors into placing in the gun during the Russian roulette torture?

ABOUT THIS MOVIE

At the Academy Awards ceremony where this celebrated film about war and friendship won Best Picture, the Oscar was appropriately presented by John Wayne in one of his last public appearances. Additionally, when the Italian-American director won his Best Director Oscar, it was presented to "my fellow paisan" by Francis Ford Coppola.

Answers • Who? John Cazale, George Dzundza, Robert De Niro, John Savage **What?** The Deer Hunter **When?** 1978 **Who?** Michael Cimino
Trivia answer 1 They were steelworkers
Trivia answer 2 Drops of wine spilling on the bride's dress
Trivia answer 3 Three

PICTURE TRIVIA

5 POINTS per actor — **Who** are the actors in this film?

5 POINTS — **What** is the title of this film?

5 POINTS — **When** was this film released?

5 POINTS — **Who** is the director of this film?

BONUS TRIVIA

10 POINTS — What real-life famous comedian was performing at the Copacabana when Jimmy took Karen there on their first date?

10 POINTS — What were the two lessons Jimmy learned after his first arrest?

10 POINTS — Which airline heist turned out to be their biggest score?

ABOUT THIS MOVIE

Like the real-life character who broke the rules of his gangster life in this film, the director broke cinematic rules to tell the story. Multiple narrative voices, shifting points of view, characters speaking directly to the camera, and a rousing pop/rock soundtrack spanning the four decades across which this tale of mobsters unfolds are some examples.

Answers • Who? Ray Liotta, Joe Pesci, Catherine Scorsese, Robert De Niro **What?** GoodFellas **When?** 1990 **Who?** Martin Scorsese
Trivia answer 1 Henny Youngman
Trivia answer 2 Never rat on your friends and always keep your mouth shut
Trivia answer 3 The Lufthansa heist

PICTURE TRIVIA

WHO WHAT WHEN & WHERE

5 POINTS per actor — **Who** are the actors in this film?

5 POINTS — **What** is the title of this film?

5 POINTS — **When** was this film released?

5 POINTS — **Who** is the director of this film?

BONUS TRIVIA

10 POINTS — What time did the alarm clock wake Phil every morning?

10 POINTS — Did Punxsutawney Phil see his shadow?

10 POINTS — What did Phil sculpt in the ice for Rita?

Rarely have eastern philosophy and western comedy been stitched so seamlessly together as in this film about a bored weatherman finding himself tortured daily with the opportunity to do things over again. Embraced by the general moviegoing audience as well as Buddhists and Yogis in equal measure, the unique accomplishment of this film was its ability to strike a rare balance between comedy and existentialism, an American holiday and a personal spiritual journey.

Answers • Who? Bill Murray, Andie MacDowell **What?** Groundhog Day **When?** 1993 **Who?** Harold Ramis
Trivia answer 1 6 a.m.
Trivia answer 2 Yes
Trivia answer 3 Her face

PICTURE TRIVIA

WHO WHAT WHEN & WHERE

5 POINTS per actor — **Who** are the actors in this film?

5 POINTS — **What** is the title of this film?

5 POINTS — **When** was this film released?

5 POINTS — **Who** is the director of this film?

BONUS TRIVIA

10 POINTS — What was Annie's objection to Paul's writing in his newest manuscript?

10 POINTS — Which letter was missing from the used typewriter Annie bought for Paul?

10 POINTS — Who was Annie's all-time favorite musician?

ABOUT THIS MOVIE

Only a writer of horror could write a story about what is possibly a writer's worst nightmare; and only Stephen King could write such a story and have it become a bestseller before being adapted into this film. The notorious "hobbling" scene in the book was toned down (relatively speaking) for the film version, to the objection of the screenwriter, until he finally saw the finished film and realized that the scene as written—in the book as well as in his screenplay—would likely have been too horrifying for the general audience.

Answers • Who? Kathy Bates, James Caan **What?** Misery **When?** 1990 **Who?** Rob Reiner
Trivia answer 1 The profanity
Trivia answer 2 N
Trivia answer 3 Liberace

PICTURE TRIVIA

WHO WHAT WHEN & WHERE

5 POINTS per actor — **Who** are the actors in this film?

5 POINTS — **What** is the title of this film?

5 POINTS — **When** was this film released?

5 POINTS — **Who** is the director of this film?

BONUS TRIVIA

10 POINTS — What was the pizzeria's slogan, seen on all the employees' shirts?

10 POINTS — Which university was Kat accepted into?

10 POINTS — What rating did the Fireside Gourmet food critic give the pizzeria?

ABOUT THIS MOVIE

A trio of actresses, little known at the time, carried this story about two sisters and their friend in a seaport town in Connecticut. All three have gone on to greater heights in their careers. Kat portrayed Dana Scully's successor Monica Reyes in the last two seasons of "X-Files"; Jojo became a renowned character actress; and Daisy attained international stardom two years later as the star of "Pretty Woman."

Answers • Who? Julia Roberts **What?** Mystic Pizza **When?** 1988 **Who?** Donald Petrie
Trivia answer 1 A Slice of Heaven
Trivia answer 2 Yale
Trivia answer 3 Four stars for "superb"

PICTURE TRIVIA

WHO WHAT WHEN & WHERE

5 POINTS per actor — **Who** are the actors in this film?

5 POINTS — **What** is the title of this film?

5 POINTS — **When** was this film released?

5 POINTS — **Who** is the director of this film?

BONUS TRIVIA

10 POINTS — What was the name of Rick's piano player?

10 POINTS — Where did Rick hide the Letters of Transit?

10 POINTS — What was the rigged roulette number that hit twice in a row, allowing the Bulgarian couple to win enough cash to leave?

ABOUT THIS MOVIE

For the rest of her life the actress who played Ilsa Lund could not understand why this film had become such a favorite of her fans. She always described it as a "nice movie" but was amazed at its continuing popularity. It was a studio film, shot in a few weeks, and completely forgotten by cast and crew until it won the Best Picture Oscar in 1943.

Answers • Who? Humphrey Bogart, Ingrid Bergman **What?** Casablanca **When?** 1942 **Who?** Michael Curtiz
Trivia answer 1 Sam
Trivia answer 2 Under the lid of the piano
Trivia answer 3 22

PICTURE TRIVIA

WHO WHAT WHEN & WHERE

5 POINTS per actor — **Who** are the actors in this film?

5 POINTS — **What** is the title of this film?

5 POINTS — **When** was this film released?

5 POINTS — **Who** is the director of this film?

BONUS TRIVIA

10 POINTS — What did Lloyd and Harry do for their respective livings?

10 POINTS — Where did Lloyd and Harry head off to in search of the woman Lloyd drove to the airport?

10 POINTS — What kind of bird was Harry's pet, the one whose head "fell off"?

ABOUT THIS MOVIE

This film was the third straight hit for its star (following "Ace Ventura: Pet Detective" and "The Mask"), propelling him from struggling actor to stardom in a single year. As if that wasn't enough, he would soon make a new record for himself as the first actor to be paid $20 million — to star in "The Cable Guy."

Answers • Who? Jim Carrey, Jeff Daniels **What?** Dumb and Dumber **When?** 1994 **Who?** Peter and Bobby Farrelly
Trivia answer 1 Lloyd was a limo driver; Harry was a pet groomer
Trivia answer 2 Aspen, Colorado
Trivia answer 3 A parakeet

PICTURE TRIVIA

5 POINTS per actor — **Who** are the actors in this film?

5 POINTS — **What** is the title of this film?

5 POINTS — **When** was this film released?

5 POINTS — **Who** is the director of this film?

BONUS TRIVIA

10 POINTS — What did the landowner do to Joseph's family farm on the day of their father's burial?

10 POINTS — In what U.S. territory did the great land rush occur?

10 POINTS — What treasure did Shannon take with her to pay for her way in America?

ABOUT THIS MOVIE

This epic tale of Irish immigrants near the end of the nineteenth century was filmed in widescreen 70 millimeter format, capturing the gorgeous vistas of rural Ireland, the vast U.S. plains, and the overcrowded streets of Boston —though the scenes in old Boston were actually shot in Dublin.

Answers • Who? Nicole Kidman, Tom Cruise **What?** Far and Away **When?** 1992 **Who?** Ron Howard
Trivia answer 1 Burned it to the ground
Trivia answer 2 Oklahoma Territory
Trivia answer 3 A family collection of antique silver spoons

PICTURETRIVIA

WHO WHAT WHEN & WHERE

5 POINTS per actor — **Who** are the actors in this film?

5 POINTS — **What** is the title of this film?

5 POINTS — **When** was this film released?

5 POINTS — **Who** is the director of this film?

BONUSTRIVIA

10 POINTS — What did his older sister leave Billy under his bed when she left home?

10 POINTS — What was the name of the band Billy went on tour with?

10 POINTS — What did Penny Lane call girls like her and not "groupies"?

ABOUT THIS MOVIE

To appear as authentically real on film as an actual Seventies rock band, the actors who portrayed the lead guitarist and front man for the fictional band in this story were mentored on guitar and performance by none other than iconic Seventies musician Peter Frampton. And for them to play music that could only have come from that time period, the director consulted with Nancy Wilson, formerly of "Heart," (and also the director's wife).

Answers • Who? Patrick Fugit, Kate Hudson **What?** Almost Famous **When?** 2000 **Who?** Cameron Crowe
Trivia answer 1 Her record collection
Trivia answer 2 Stillwater
Trivia answer 3 Band aids

PICTURE TRIVIA

WHO WHAT WHEN & WHERE

⑤ **Who** are the actors in this film?
POINTS per actor

⑤ **What** is the title of this film?
POINTS

⑤ **When** was this film released?
POINTS

⑤ **Who** is the director of this film?
POINTS

BONUS TRIVIA

10 Where did Lester set up
POINTS his gym equipment?

10 What was the name of the
POINTS fast food restaurant where
Lester found work?

10 What was the name of the
POINTS advertising magazine for
which Lester first worked?

ABOUT THIS MOVIE

Among the many possible meanings of this film's title, an additional one could well reflect the work of cinematographer Conrad Hall, whose films have also included "Butch Cassidy and the Sundance Kid" and "In Cold Blood." Hall began his career filming episodes of the classic black & white television series, "The Outer Limits."

Answers • Who? Annette Bening, Kevin Spacey **What?** American Beauty **When?** 1999 **Who?** Sam Mendes
Trivia answer 1 In the garage
Trivia answer 2 Mr. Smiley's
Trivia answer 3 "Media Monthly"

PICTURE TRIVIA

WHO WHAT WHEN & WHERE

⑤ **Who** are the actors in this film?
POINTS per actor

⑤ **What** is the title of this film?
POINTS

⑤ **When** was this film released?
POINTS

⑤ **Who** is the director of this film?
POINTS

BONUS TRIVIA

10 What was the stage name
POINTS that Albert used when he
performed at the club?

10 What country was Agador
POINTS Spartacus from?

10 What party and state
POINTS did Senator Kevin Keeley
represent?

A remake of a 1978 French farce, this equally successful film transplants the characters to South Beach in Miami but otherwise keeps the story and situations fairly intact. A documentary about drag queens was created for the express purpose of teaching the stars how to portray their roles.

Answers • Who? Nathan Lane, Robin Williams **What?** The Birdcage **When?** 1996 **Who?** Mike Nichols
Trivia answer 1 Starina
Trivia answer 2 Guatemala
Trivia answer 3 He was a Republican from Ohio

PICTURE TRIVIA

WHO WHAT WHEN & WHERE

5 POINTS per actor — **Who** are the actors in this film?

5 POINTS — **What** is the title of this film?

5 POINTS — **When** was this film released?

5 POINTS — **Who** is the director of this film?

BONUS TRIVIA

10 POINTS — What did Dr. Larch fondly call all the kids in his orphanage at their bedtimes?

10 POINTS — How did Homer finally get rid of the piece of paper with the rules on it?

10 POINTS — What movie was playing on movie night at the orphanage?

ABOUT THIS MOVIE

Normally the author of an original novel is the last person chosen to write the screenplay to be adapted from it, because the need to compress the story and delete so much is usually too painful a task for most authors. In the case of this film, however, the novelist took it upon himself to take his 500+ page novel and pare it down to a workable two-hour film.

Answers • **Who?** Tobey Maguire, Charlize Theron **What?** The Cider House Rules **When?** 1999 **Who?** Lasse Hallström
Trivia answer **1** "You princes of Maine, you kings of New England"
Trivia answer **2** He threw it into the stove
Trivia answer **3** "King Kong"

PICTURE TRIVIA

WHO WHAT WHEN & WHERE

5 POINTS per actor — **Who** are the actors in this film?

5 POINTS — **What** is the title of this film?

5 POINTS — **When** was this film released?

5 POINTS — **Who** is the director of this film?

BONUS TRIVIA

10 POINTS — What did the assistant DA say Catherine was not allowed to do in the interrogation room?

10 POINTS — What was the name of Catherine's novel?

10 POINTS — What was the unwanted nickname Internal Affairs had given to Nick?

ABOUT THIS MOVIE

Somewhat patterned after "Vertigo," but with huge dollops of sex and violence, this tale of a murderess incited angry demonstrations and a campaign of denunciation by the gay and lesbian community in San Francisco for what it considered to be another denigrating portrayal of a bisexual character as psychotic and homicidal. The publicity served both camps, as the film was one of the biggest hits of the year, and the ensuing dialogue laid the foundation for a greater range and sensitivity in film and television shows today.

Answers • Who? Sharon Stone, Michael Douglas **What?** Basic Instinct **When?** 1992 **Who?** Paul Verhoeven
Trivia answer 1 Smoke
Trivia answer 2 "Love Hurts"
Trivia answer 3 Shooter

PICTURE TRIVIA

WHO WHAT WHEN & WHERE

5 POINTS per actor — **Who** are the actors in this film?

5 POINTS — **What** is the title of this film?

5 POINTS — **When** was this film released?

5 POINTS — **Who** is the director of this film?

BONUS TRIVIA

10 POINTS — What did Moses buy Addie in the diner while waiting for the train to St. Joseph?

10 POINTS — What did Moses sell door to door?

10 POINTS — Where did Moses and Addie keep their money?

ABOUT THIS MOVIE

Filmed in the grand old style of films of the Thirties and Forties, with long takes, full depth-of-field, and red and green filters to accentuate the contrast in the sky (as in the classic westerns of John Ford), this Depression-era story featured a real father and daughter team. The actress who played Addie was only eight-and-a-half-years old at the time, and smoked non-tobacco "lettuce cigarettes" as part of her role as a tough and clever little cookie.

Answers • Who? Ryan O'Neal, Tatum O'Neal **What?** Paper Moon **When?** 1973 **Who?** Peter Bogdanovich
Trivia answer 1 A Coney Island and a Nehi (a hot dog and a soft drink)
Trivia answer 2 Bibles
Trivia answer 3 In a Cremo brand cigar box

PICTURE TRIVIA

5 POINTS per actor — **Who** are the actors in this film?

5 POINTS — **What** is the title of this film?

5 POINTS — **When** was this film released?

5 POINTS — **Who** is the director of this film?

BONUS TRIVIA

10 POINTS — Why did the IRA kidnap Jody?

10 POINTS — What game did Jody play and consider to be the best game in the world?

10 POINTS — What did Dil give Fergus during their first meeting?

ABOUT THIS MOVIE

Containing one of the most well known story twists in recent movie history, this film was shot on a shoestring budget without any major stars. To help conceal the surprise, the name of the person who played Dil was modified slightly in the credits to increase the ambiguity of the character.

Answers • Who? Forest Whitaker, Stephen Rea **What?** The Crying Game **When?** 1992 **Who?** Neil Jordan
Trivia answer 1 To trade him for an IRA member being held by the British
Trivia answer 2 Cricket
Trivia answer 3 A haircut

PICTURETRIVIA

⑤ **Who** are the actors in this film?
POINTS per actor

⑤ **What** is the title of this film?
POINTS

⑤ **When** was this film released?
POINTS

⑤ **Who** is the director of this film?
POINTS

BONUSTRIVIA

10 What musical instrument
POINTS did Jane play?

10 How many kids did
POINTS Sukie have?

10 What was the name of
POINTS Daryl Van Horne's butler?

ABOUT THIS MOVIE

There is something about New England and the supernatural that seem to go together naturally, but a suitable real town to stand in for the town of this film's title was searched for far and wide before one was finally discovered in the most appropriate place; the scenic New England coastal village of Cohasset, where much of this film was shot, is just an hour south of that other witchy place — Salem, Massachusetts.

Answers • Who? Cher, Susan Sarandon, Michelle Pfeiffer **What?** The Witches of Eastwick **When?** 1987 **Who?** George Miller
Trivia answer 1 The cello
Trivia answer 2 Six
Trivia answer 3 Fidel

PICTURE TRIVIA

WHO WHAT WHEN & WHERE

⑤ **Who** are the actors in this film?
POINTS per actor

⑤ **What** is the title of this film?
POINTS

⑤ **When** was this film released?
POINTS

⑤ **Who** is the director of this film?
POINTS

BONUS TRIVIA

🔟 About which classic movie did the actors have a running conversation for years?
POINTS

🔟 What was Sally's career goal?
POINTS

🔟 Out of what was the coffee table (that Marie and Jess were in disagreement about) designed?
POINTS

ABOUT THIS MOVIE

The most well known scene in this film (hint: the female lead pretends to have an experience you don't normally expect to have in a diner) took an entire day and dozens of takes from different angles to complete. The patron with perhaps the biggest laugh line ("I'll have what she's having") was played by the director's own mother.

PICTURE TRIVIA

WHO WHAT WHEN & WHERE

5 POINTS per actor — **Who** are the actors in this film?

5 POINTS — **What** is the title of this film?

5 POINTS — **When** was this film released?

5 POINTS — **Who** is the director of this film?

BONUS TRIVIA

10 POINTS — What was the one thing Vivian wouldn't do for a trick?

10 POINTS — What state did Vivian grow up in?

10 POINTS — How much did Vivian and Edward negotiate that he would pay for her to stay with him the full week?

ABOUT THIS MOVIE

Very few actors enjoy the privilege of becoming associated with a song, a phrase, or an iconic theme that not only defines their persona to the public but also launches their career. The star of this film achieved all of that playing the Cinderella role in this story of a millionaire businessman and the streetwalker he meets one night.

Answers • Who? Richard Gere, Julia Roberts **What?** Pretty Woman **When?** 1990 **Who?** Garry Marshall
Trivia answer 1 Kiss on the mouth
Trivia answer 2 Georgia
Trivia answer 3 $3000

PICTURETRIVIA

WHO WHAT WHEN & WHERE

5 POINTS per actor — **Who** are the actors in this film?

5 POINTS — **What** is the title of this film?

5 POINTS — **When** was this film released?

5 POINTS — **Who** is the director of this film?

BONUSTRIVIA

10 POINTS — What did Michael Dorsey change his name to for his female persona?

10 POINTS — In what famous New York City restaurant did Michael surprise his agent with his new persona?

10 POINTS — What was the name of the soap opera which Michael auditioned for as a woman — and got the part?

ABOUT THIS MOVIE

Truly a role that required a complete makeover for an actor, this film followed in the high-heeled footsteps of the classic Billy Wilder comedy "Some Like It Hot" for stories about men masquerading as women. The star was coached by a female impersonator and affected a Southern accent for the character because he wasn't able to maintain the semblance of a female pitch without it.

Answers • Who? Dustin Hoffman, Jessica Lange **What?** Tootsie **When?** 1982 **Who?** Sydney Pollack
Trivia answer 1 Dorothy Michaels
Trivia answer 2 The Russian Tea Room
Trivia answer 3 "Southwest General"

PICTURE TRIVIA

WHO WHAT WHEN & WHERE

5 POINTS per actor — **Who** are the actors in this film?

5 POINTS — **What** is the title of this film?

5 POINTS — **When** was this film released?

5 POINTS — **Who** is the director of this film?

BONUS TRIVIA

10 POINTS — What gift did the Kid get in the diner after he rescued Tess?

10 POINTS — What was the name of the club where Breathless Mahoney sang?

10 POINTS — What did the Kid choose as his legal name?

ABOUT THIS MOVIE

The title character of this film debuted in a comic strip which became a mainstay for a slate of B movies beginning in the 1940s. Nearly 60 years after the strip's debut, this big budget production generated an impressive realization of a cartoon universe in a live-action movie. The film stuck to its newspaper origins by keeping the art direction, production design, and costuming restricted to the original printing colors of the "funny papers" of the 1930s.

Answers • Who? Warren Beatty **What?** Dick Tracy **When?** 1990 **Who?** Warren Beatty
Trivia answer 1 A wristwatch radio, just like Tracy's
Trivia answer 2 Club Ritz
Trivia answer 3 Dick Tracy

PICTURE TRIVIA

5 POINTS per actor — **Who** are the actors in this film?

5 POINTS — **What** is the title of this film?

5 POINTS — **When** was this film released?

5 POINTS — **Who** is the director of this film?

BONUS TRIVIA

10 POINTS — What was the name of Joe's family's bookstore chain?

10 POINTS — What were Joe's and Kathleen's email monikers?

10 POINTS — What was the name of Joe's dog?

ABOUT THIS MOVIE

Like real estate, some films benefit greatly from location, location, location. Famous sites on the upper west side of New York City were used for many scenes in this film, though the centerpiece of the story — the big book chain that invades the neighborhood — had to be created. Failing to find a real bookstore chain that would allow filming on their property, a recently vacated Barney's clothing store was found and dressed to look like a vast book superstore.

Answers • **Who?** Tom Hanks, Meg Ryan **What?** You've Got Mail **When?** 1998 **Who?** Nora Ephron
Trivia answer 1 Fox & Sons Books
Trivia answer 2 NY152 (to indicate Joe's apartment address) and Shopgirl (for Kathleen's occupation)
Trivia answer 3 Brinkley

PICTURE TRIVIA

5 POINTS per actor — **Who** are the actors in this film?

5 POINTS — **What** is the title of this film?

5 POINTS — **When** was this film released?

5 POINTS — **Who** is the director of this film?

BONUS TRIVIA

10 POINTS — Which real-life author did the lead character run into at a book signing?

10 POINTS — Which "year of being single" was the lead character in at the start of the story?

10 POINTS — What were the guests supposed to dress up as at Uncle Geoffrey's fancy dress party?

ABOUT THIS MOVIE

It's not every day that an American actress from Texas snags the role of a truly British character made famous by a best-selling novel. A daring and much criticized choice at the time, the star of this film won over the critics by delivering a spot-on British accent and filling her role so completely that she made the title character her own.

Answers • Who? Renée Zellweger, Hugh Grant **What?** Bridget Jones's Diary **When?** 2001 **Who?** Sharon Maguire
Trivia answer 1 Salman Rushdie
Trivia answer 2 32nd
Trivia answer 3 Tarts and vicars

PICTURE TRIVIA

WHO WHAT WHEN & WHERE

⑤ POINTS per actor — **Who** are the actors in this film?

⑤ POINTS — **What** is the title of this film?

⑤ POINTS — **When** was this film released?

⑤ POINTS — **Who** is the director of this film?

BONUS TRIVIA

10 POINTS — What was the term given for the "disciplinary engagement" that led to Santiago's death?

10 POINTS — Where did the disciplinary engagement occur?

10 POINTS — What was the specific physical cause of Private Santiago's death?

For reasons unknown and circumstances unpredictable, isolated lines of dialogue from movies worm their way into the general culture and blossom into popular catchphrases. "Use the force" and "Resistance is futile" are two examples. In this film, the line, "You can't handle the truth!" took off in such a big way that it returns one of the highest number of matches for a film quote on Internet search engines.

Answers • Who? Kevin Pollak, Tom Cruise, Wolfgang Bodison, James Marshall **What?** A Few Good Men **When?** 1992 **Who?** Rob Reiner
Trivia answer 1 Code Red
Trivia answer 2 The U.S. Naval Base at Guantanamo Bay, Cuba
Trivia answer 3 Asphyxiation brought on by acute lactic acidosis

PICTURE TRIVIA

WHO WHAT WHEN & WHERE

(5) POINTS per actor **Who** are the actors in this film?

(5) POINTS **What** is the title of this film?

(5) POINTS **When** was this film released?

(5) POINTS **Who** is the director of this film?

BONUS TRIVIA

10 POINTS In which state was the Kinsella farm?

10 POINTS What major league baseball team did Shoeless Joe play for?

10 POINTS To which stadium did Ray take Terrence Mann to see a game?

ABOUT THIS MOVIE

Neither the cornfield nor the baseball field that were such important elements in this film were created without difficulty. A drought caused the corn to grow late and the infield grass to dry out too early. Irrigation for the corn and paint for the grass had to be used to create the needed effects. During casting for this film, no one expected that their first choice to star would want to do two baseball-themed films in a row (he had just completed "Bull Durham"), but when the script found its way to him, he eagerly accepted the role.

Answers • Who? Burt Lancaster, Gaby Hoffman, Kevin Costner **What?** Field of Dreams **When?** 1989 **Who?** Phil Alden Robinson
Trivia answer 1 Iowa
Trivia answer 2 The Chicago White Sox
Trivia answer 3 Fenway Park

PICTURETRIVIA

⑤ **Who** are the actors in this film?
POINTS per actor

⑤ **What** is the title of this film?
POINTS

⑤ **When** was this film released?
POINTS

⑤ **Who** is the director of this film?
POINTS

BONUSTRIVIA

10 What was the actual thing "Rosebud" designated?
POINTS

10 What was the name of Charles' magnificent palatial estate?
POINTS

10 What real person was the story based on?
POINTS

ABOUT THIS MOVIE

Herman Mankiewicz, the screenwriter, was once a guest at a well known publishing magnate's vast party-hearty compound (San Simeon) where the rich and famous gathered for grand weekends during the Thirties. But the host had strict rules, including no alcohol and no cursing, and apparently Mankiewicz broke at least one and was ejected. A few years later, he completed a script entitled "American," about an individual remarkably similar to his host, which ultimately became this film.

Answers • Who? Joseph Cotton, Orson Welles, Everett Sloan **What?** Citizen Kane **When?** 1941 **Who?** Orson Welles
Trivia answer 1 Kane's childhood sled
Trivia answer 2 Xanadu
Trivia answer 3 William Randolph Hearst, the publishing magnate

PICTURE TRIVIA

WHO WHAT WHEN & WHERE

5 POINTS per actor — **Who** are the actors in this film?

5 POINTS — **What** is the title of this film?

5 POINTS — **When** was this film released?

5 POINTS — **Who** is the director of this film?

BONUS TRIVIA

10 POINTS — At which university did the story take place?

10 POINTS — What request of Skylar's drove the lead character away from her?

10 POINTS — What kind of math problem did Professor Lambeau put on the main hallway chalkboard as a challenge for his students?

ABOUT THIS MOVIE

Of the many paths to success in Hollywood, one of the most unusual ones was taken by the two actors/writers of this film. Friends growing up, they wrote the screenplay together as a vehicle for themselves. Early drafts had a stronger spy element involving the NSA, which industry mentors like Rob Reiner and William Goldman advised they downplay in favor of the more personal elements in the story. Eventually their script went on to win an Oscar for Best Original Screenplay and launched both their careers.

Answers • Who? Minnie Driver, Matt Damon, Ben Affleck **What?** Good Will Hunting **When?** 1997 **Who?** Gus Van Sant
Trivia answer 1 MIT
Trivia answer 2 To come with her to California
Trivia answer 3 An advanced Fourier system problem

PICTURE TRIVIA

WHO WHAT WHEN & WHERE

5 POINTS per actor — **Who** are the actors in this film?

5 POINTS — **What** is the title of this film?

5 POINTS — **When** was this film released?

5 POINTS — **Who** is the director of this film?

BONUS TRIVIA

10 POINTS — Which notorious gangster's arrest caused the criminal power vacuum in 1950s Los Angeles?

10 POINTS — Which movie star did Ed Exley mistake for a prostitute?

10 POINTS — What was Sid Hudgens' closing line for all the articles he wrote for his celebrity tabloid?

ABOUT THIS MOVIE

Novelist James Ellroy's dense, violent, and dark novel of cops and killers in 1950s Los Angeles provided more than enough story grist for the Hollywood mill. One of the challenges in the making of this film was to visually recreate that singular time period depicting both its sleazy and glamorous faces. Ironically, the three major leads were filled by two Australians and a kid from New Jersey.

Answers • Who? Danny DeVito, Kevin Spacey **What?** L.A. Confidential **When?** 1997 **Who?** Curtis Hanson
Trivia answer 1 Mickey Cohen
Trivia answer 2 Lana Turner
Trivia answer 3 "You heard it here first, off the record, on the 'QT,' and very hush-hush"

PICTURE TRIVIA

5 POINTS per actor — **Who** are the actors in this film?

5 POINTS — **What** is the title of this film?

5 POINTS — **When** was this film released?

5 POINTS — **Who** is the director of this film?

BONUS TRIVIA

10 POINTS — Where was the main entrance to the alien policing organization?

10 POINTS — How many aliens are living on earth at any one time (and mostly in New York)?

10 POINTS — What kind of weapon did Jeebs the pawnbroker sell to the assassin that Agent J ran down?

ABOUT THIS MOVIE

Based on a comic book series that was itself loosely based on the urban legend of mysterious agents fighting otherworldly creatures, this film went through a fairly long development process to get to the big screen. But 20 years after the first "Star Wars" film took place, a long time ago in a galaxy far, far away, this film brought its own population of cute, clever, or dangerous alien creatures to this planet, right here and right now.

Answers • Who? Will Smith, Rip Torn, Tommy Lee Jones **What?** Men in Black **When?** 1997 **Who?** Barry Sonnenfeld
Trivia answer 1 The Battery Tunnel Authority in New York City
Trivia answer 2 About 1500
Trivia answer 3 A reverberating carbonizer with mutate capacity

PICTURE TRIVIA

WHO WHAT WHEN & WHERE

5 POINTS per actor **Who** are the actors in this film?

5 POINTS **What** is the title of this film?

5 POINTS **When** was this film released?

5 POINTS **Who** is the director of this film?

BONUS TRIVIA

10 POINTS What was the name the three fugitives used in their guise as a traveling music group?

10 POINTS What did Tommy Johnson sell to get good with the guitar?

10 POINTS What was Ulysses' favorite brand of pomade hair treatment?

ABOUT THIS MOVIE

While this film's story took place during the great droughts of the Thirties that inflicted most of the American South and Midwest, the principal photography for the film took place in midsummer. Hence the imagery caught on film had to be digitally manipulated to turn the lush greens and thick foliage of a humid summer in the South into the browns and tans of the dust bowl during the Depression.

Answers • Who? John Turturro, Tim Blake Nelson, George Clooney **What?** O Brother, Where Art Thou? **When?** 2000 **Who?** Joel and Ethan Coen
Trivia answer 1 The Soggy Bottom Boys
Trivia answer 2 His soul (to the devil)
Trivia answer 3 Dapper Dan

PICTURE TRIVIA

WHO WHAT WHEN & WHERE

5 POINTS per actor — **Who** are the actors in this film?

5 POINTS — **What** is the title of this film?

5 POINTS — **When** was this film released?

5 POINTS — **Who** is the director of this film?

BONUS TRIVIA

10 POINTS — What was the working title of the play William was suffering writer's block over?

10 POINTS — What idiosyncratic habit did Will give in to before sitting down to write?

10 POINTS — What was the name of the rival theater run by Richard Burbage?

ABOUT THIS MOVIE

To achieve the authenticity of Elizabethan England for this film, the street exteriors were dressed with mud, dirt, and even horse manure. But an actual place for the famous balcony scene, with all the necessary elements—balcony, garden, and vines strong enough to climb—in a single location couldn't be found. So the shots for the balcony, a constructed set, had to be photographed separately from the shots in a real garden and then edited together to look like a single location.

Answers • Who? Joseph Fiennes, Gwyneth Paltrow **What?** Shakespeare in Love **When?** 1998 **Who?** John Madden
Trivia answer 1 "Romeo and Ethel, the Sea Pirate's Daughter"
Trivia answer 2 He rolled the quill between his hands and spit
Trivia answer 3 The Curtain Theater

PICTURE TRIVIA

WHO WHAT WHEN & WHERE

- **5** POINTS per actor — **Who** are the actors in this film?
- **5** POINTS — **What** is the title of this film?
- **5** POINTS — **When** was this film released?
- **5** POINTS — **Who** is the director of this film?

BONUS TRIVIA

- **10** POINTS — How long had Leonard been in his unresponsive state?
- **10** POINTS — How many milligrams of L-Dopa were needed to revive Leonard?
- **10** POINTS — What did Leonard carve into the wooden bench when he was a boy?

ABOUT THIS MOVIE

This film was based loosely on a true story of patients suffering from a form of Parkinson's Disease contracted during an epidemic in the 1920s. The actors who played Leonard and the doctor who helped him prepared for their roles by watching films of the actual patients. One of those patients, still living at the time, appeared in the film.

Answers • Who? Robert De Niro, Robin Williams **What?** Awakenings **When?** 1990 **Who?** Penny Marshall
Trivia answer 1 30 years
Trivia answer 2 1000 milligrams (or 1 gram)
Trivia answer 3 His name

PICTURETRIVIA

⑤ **Who** are the actors in this film?
POINTS per actor

⑤ **What** is the title of this film?
POINTS

⑤ **When** was this film released?
POINTS

⑤ **Who** is the director of this film?
POINTS

BONUSTRIVIA

10 In which Eastern
POINTS European city did the initial mission go bad?

10 What was the mysterious
POINTS Max's line of work?

10 What was the name of the
POINTS coded file stolen from the National Security Agency?

ABOUT THIS MOVIE

Successful adaptations require a careful mix of the old and the new. This movie adaptation of the Sixties TV show of the same name combined a contemporary plot of international intrigue with the classic trappings from the original show: impersonation via face masks, futuristic gadgetry, and a famous preview of things to come while a burning fuse grows ever shorter.

Answers • Who? Tom Cruise, Jean Reno **What?** Mission: Impossible **When?** 1996 **Who?** Brian De Palma
Trivia answer 1 Prague
Trivia answer 2 Arms dealing
Trivia answer 3 The NOC (Non Official Cover) list

PICTURE TRIVIA

(5) POINTS per actor — **Who** are the actors in this film?

(5) POINTS — **What** is the title of this film?

(5) POINTS — **When** was this film released?

(5) POINTS — **Who** is the director of this film?

BONUS TRIVIA

10 POINTS — What was the first thing to appear in color in the town?

10 POINTS — What was the name of the high school basketball team?

10 POINTS — What was the name of the television network that broadcast only old black & white TV shows?

ABOUT THIS MOVIE

Shooting in color requires different lighting techniques than shooting in black & white, so making a film where black & white and color were mixed together in some shots proved a challenge. Tricks such as changing the lighting intensity on an individual in color entering a black & white environment, using makeup that was transparent in black & white but not in color, and digitally adjusting color elements to better blend in with black & white elements were all used to create the seamless — if highly unusual — world of this story.

Answers • Who? Tobey Maguire, Reese Witherspoon **What?** Pleasantville **When?** 1998 **Who?** Gary Ross
Trivia answer 1 A red rose
Trivia answer 2 The (Undefeated) Pleasantville Lions
Trivia answer 3 TV Time

PICTURETRIVIA

WHO WHAT WHEN & WHERE

5 POINTS per actor — **Who** are the actors in this film?

5 POINTS — **What** is the title of this film?

5 POINTS — **When** was this film released?

5 POINTS — **Who** is the director of this film?

BONUSTRIVIA

10 POINTS — How many times in a row did Melvin have to flick the light switch or turn the locks on doors?

10 POINTS — What behavior did Simon's dog Verdell share with Melvin Udall?

10 POINTS — What did Carol's son Spencer suffer from?

This film brought both its leads Academy Awards, an accomplishment that has happened regularly but not often, only seven times for seven films in Oscar history, and only one actor — the male lead in this film — has been a recipient under these circumstances twice.

Answers • Who? Jack Nicholson, Greg Kinnear **What?** As Good As It Gets **When?** 1997 **Who?** James L. Brooks
Trivia answer 1 Five
Trivia answer 2 The compulsion to avoid stepping on cracks in the sidewalk
Trivia answer 3 A severe form of asthma

PICTURETRIVIA

WHOWHATWHEN&WHERE

⑤ **Who** are the actors in this film?
POINTS per actor

⑤ **What** is the title of this film?
POINTS

⑤ **When** was this film released?
POINTS

⑤ **Who** is the director of this film?
POINTS

BONUSTRIVIA

10 What was David Dunn's profession?
POINTS

10 What was David's one vulnerability (like Kryptonite for Superman)?
POINTS

10 From what bone disease did Elijah Price suffer?
POINTS

ABOUT THIS MOVIE

In his previous work, the director of this film used specific colors to signify and symbolize certain elements of the story. In this film he again used color, but this time to show the psychic connectedness the main character had with strangers he came in contact with.

Answers • Who? Bruce Willis, Samuel L. Jackson **What?** Unbreakable **When?** 2000 **Who?** M. Night Shyamalan
Trivia answer 1 Security guard at a sports stadium
Trivia answer 2 Water
Trivia answer 3 Osteogenesis Imperfecta

PICTURE TRIVIA

5 POINTS per actor — **Who** are the actors in this film?

5 POINTS — **What** is the title of this film?

5 POINTS — **When** was this film released?

5 POINTS — **Who** is the director of this film?

BONUS TRIVIA

10 POINTS — According to Stanley, what was the main tenet of the "Napoleonic Code"?

10 POINTS — What subject did Blanche DuBois once teach?

10 POINTS — To get to her sister's place, which streetcar did Blanche have to transfer to?

ABOUT THIS MOVIE

The Legion of Decency (a Catholic church oversight council that had a powerful influence on the film industry's own regulatory body, the Hays Commission) forced the director to excise several scenes from this film. But the powerful performances of the cast and the sultry atmosphere of the film made it all the more erotic and dangerous for what it couldn't show explicitly. A recent DVD release restores a number of the censored scenes.

Answers • Who? Marlon Brando, Vivien Leigh **What?** A Streetcar Named Desire **When?** 1951 **Who?** Elia Kazan
Trivia answer 1 What belongs to the wife belongs to the husband
Trivia answer 2 English
Trivia answer 3 The streetcar named "Cemetery"

PICTURE TRIVIA

WHO WHAT WHEN & WHERE

5 POINTS per actor — **Who** are the actors in this film?

5 POINTS — **What** is the title of this film?

5 POINTS — **When** was this film released?

5 POINTS — **Who** is the director of this film?

BONUS TRIVIA

10 POINTS — What was the Secret Service's code name for referring to President Shepherd?

10 POINTS — How many votes did Sydney need to get for the fossil fuel bill in order for the President to provide his full support?

10 POINTS — Which country did President Shepherd order the bombing of, in response to their bombing of secret American assets?

ABOUT THIS MOVIE

Even though filming in and around the White House, the Capitol, and at Camp David was out of the question, the director and members of the crew of this film were given unusual and privileged access to accompany then President Clinton for a number of days to observe in detail the environment he worked in. The scene of the President's entrance into Congress to give the State of the Union address was not filmed there, but was instead a completely realistic special effects composite.

Answers • Who? Michael Douglas **What?** The American President **When?** 1995 **Who?** Rob Reiner
Trivia answer 1 Liberty
Trivia answer 2 24
Trivia answer 3 Libya

PICTURE TRIVIA

WHO WHAT WHEN & WHERE

⑤ **Who** are the actors in this film?
POINTS per actor

⑤ **What** is the title of this film?
POINTS

⑤ **When** was this film released?
POINTS

⑤ **Who** is the director of this film?
POINTS

BONUS TRIVIA

10 How much did Mrs. Wilkinson
POINTS charge for her ballet lessons?

10 Unable to afford coal,
POINTS what cherished household
item did the father break
into firewood for heat
during the winter?

10 Which ballet did the lead
POINTS character debut in as an
adult?

Culture clashes can happen within the same household, according to this film — which tells the story of a family pulled apart by political and financial turmoil during the highly disruptive and painful British miners' strike of the mid-Eighties. Over 2,000 boys auditioned for the lead, which required someone who could dance, act, and who was from the northeast of England so that he would have the correct regional accent for the role.

Answers • Who? Jamie Bell **What?** Billy Elliot **When?** 2000 **Who?** Stephen Daldry
Trivia answer 1 50p (pence) per class
Trivia answer 2 The family piano
Trivia answer 3 "Swan Lake"

PICTURE TRIVIA

WHO WHAT WHEN & WHERE

5 POINTS per actor — **Who** are the actors in this film?

5 POINTS — **What** is the title of this film?

5 POINTS — **When** was this film released?

5 POINTS — **Who** is the director of this film?

BONUS TRIVIA

10 POINTS — Which side of Verbal Kint's body was debilitated?

10 POINTS — What was Keyser Soze's country of origin?

10 POINTS — According to Verbal, what was the greatest trick the devil ever pulled?

ABOUT THIS MOVIE

Deceptive to the nth degree, this film introduced the world to the elusive Keyser Soze, a fictional character as well recognized now as any literary persona. Made on a relatively small budget of $6 million, this film's screenplay snared an Oscar, as well as a Best Actor award for the actor who played Verbal Kint.

Answers • Who? Gabriel Byrne, Kevin Spacey **What?** The Usual Suspects **When?** 1995 **Who?** Bryan Singer
Trivia answer 1 His left side
Trivia answer 2 Turkey
Trivia answer 3 Convincing the world he didn't exist

PICTURE TRIVIA

5 POINTS per actor — **Who** are the actors in this film?

5 POINTS — **What** is the title of this film?

5 POINTS — **When** was this film released?

5 POINTS — **Who** is the director of this film?

BONUS TRIVIA

10 POINTS — What did David call the board of directors of his company?

10 POINTS — Who did David base the persona of his psychologist upon?

10 POINTS — What was the name of the corporation David signed the contract with?

ABOUT THIS MOVIE

This film about dreams within dreams (and the line between reality and fantasy) took advantage of its photogenic star, who played on his own public persona within the context of the story. The star's character in the film was disfigured and spent a large amount of screen time wearing a mask, therefore hiding away his internationally famous face. Not only was this film a remake of a Spanish film done only a few years earlier, but the lead actress in the original repeated the same role in this American version.

Answers • Who? Tom Cruise, Penelope Cruz **What?** Vanilla Sky **When?** 2001 **Who?** Cameron Crowe
Trivia answer 1 The seven dwarves
Trivia answer 2 Gregory Peck as Atticus Finch in "To Kill a Mockingbird"
Trivia answer 3 Life Extension Corporation

PICTURE TRIVIA

WHO WHAT WHEN & WHERE

5 POINTS per actor — **Who** are the actors in this film?

5 POINTS — **What** is the title of this film?

5 POINTS — **When** was this film released?

5 POINTS — **Who** is the director of this film?

BONUS TRIVIA

10 POINTS — What was the bulky package that Clark picked up at the airport for Carmine?

10 POINTS — What original painting did Carmine purport to have hanging over the fireplace in his home in Queens?

10 POINTS — From which state did Clarke Kellogg hail?

There are many film parodies, but few where an actor pokes fun at his own previous work. In this film, the star who played the role of Carmine Sabatini revived his Oscar winning characterization of Don Corleone in "The Godfather" to comic effect.

Answers • Who? Marlon Brando, Matthew Broderick **What?** The Freshman **When?** 1990 **Who?** Andrew Bergman
Trivia answer 1 A Komodo dragon
Trivia answer 2 The Mona Lisa
Trivia answer 3 Vermont

PICTURETRIVIA

5 POINTS per actor — **Who** are the actors in this film?

5 POINTS — **What** is the title of this film?

5 POINTS — **When** was this film released?

5 POINTS — **Who** is the director of this film?

BONUSTRIVIA

10 POINTS — How did Dudley demonstrate to the Bishop that he was indeed an angel?

10 POINTS — What did the cabbie like about the attitudes of Dudley and Julia?

10 POINTS — What reassurance to a great concern did the Professor receive from Dudley?

A troubled production, several false starts, and a bad film precedent didn't bode well for this film. Sets were redesigned and rebuilt, writers came and went, and the original casting of the two leads, for Dudley the angel and the Bishop, were reversed. But when it came out a year after another film prominently featuring an angel ("It's a Wonderful Life," initially a commercial failure), this film was a commercial and critical success.

Answers • Who? Cary Grant, Loretta Young, David Niven **What?** The Bishop's Wife **When?** 1947 **Who?** Henry Koster
Trivia answer 1 By opening and closing a locked door that remained locked after he went through it and closed it again
Trivia answer 2 They knew their destination, but they were in no hurry to get there
Trivia answer 3 That he would live long enough to finish his long delayed book on the history of the Roman Empire

PICTURE TRIVIA

5 POINTS per actor — **Who** are the actors in this film?

5 POINTS — **What** is the title of this film?

5 POINTS — **When** was this film released?

5 POINTS — **Who** is the director of this film?

BONUS TRIVIA

10 POINTS — What kind of creature was Smeagol before he became Gollum?

10 POINTS — What else did Frodo part with when the Ring was destroyed?

10 POINTS — What was the name of the sword that originally cut the Ring from Sauron's hand?

ABOUT THIS MOVIE

Easily one of the most ambitious undertakings in movie history, with ample fame and precedent from the trilogy of books it was based on, the actual, literal seeds for this film were planted the year before principal photography began. The land of Hobbiton, a location picked in New Zealand, began with real landscaping and community design so that it would be an actual place and photographed as such, without the need for imagery generated by computer effects.

Answers • Who? Elijah Wood, Andy Serkis, Sean Astin **What?** The Lord of the Rings: The Return of the King **When?** 2003 **Who?** Peter Jackson
Trivia answer 1 A Hobbit
Trivia answer 2 The finger on which he was wearing the One Ring
Trivia answer 3 Narsil

PICTURE TRIVIA

WHO WHAT WHEN & WHERE

5 POINTS per actor — **Who** are the actors in this film?

5 POINTS — **What** is the title of this film?

5 POINTS — **When** was this film released?

5 POINTS — **Who** is the director of this film?

BONUS TRIVIA

10 POINTS — What was the name of Stanley's dog?

10 POINTS — What was the name of the city where Stanley lived and worked?

10 POINTS — What was the name of the park where Stanley met Tina?

ABOUT THIS MOVIE

A hyperactive combination of live action and special effects fueled this human cartoon incarnation. The comic antics of the main character "under the spell" were inspired by the cartoons of Tex Avery, who directed the classic Warner Brothers Looney Tunes cartoons and who gave life to Bugs Bunny and company.

Answers • Who? Jim Carrey, Cameron Diaz **What?** The Mask **When?** 1994 **Who?** Chuck Russell
Trivia answer 1 Milo
Trivia answer 2 Edge City
Trivia answer 3 Landfill Park

PICTURE TRIVIA

⑤ **Who** are the actors in this film?
POINTS per actor

⑤ **What** is the title of this film?
POINTS

⑤ **When** was this film released?
POINTS

⑤ **Who** is the director of this film?
POINTS

BONUS TRIVIA

10 Which artist's painting was stolen?
POINTS

10 From which museum was the painting taken?
POINTS

10 What do art insurers do before indemnifying a painting?
POINTS

ABOUT THIS MOVIE

From bank robbery to art theft, and from a Boston locale to New York City, this remake of the 1968 original changed key elements of the crime story but left intact the essential cat-and-mouse nature of the relationship between the two lead characters. One of the stars of the original appeared in a smaller role in this film.

Answers • Who? Pierce Brosnan, Rene Russo **What?** The Thomas Crown Affair **When?** 1999 **Who?** John McTiernan
Trivia answer 1 Monet
Trivia answer 2 The Metropolitan Museum of Art in New York City
Trivia answer 3 Photograph the borders of the painting (which are hidden by the frame) to compare against possible forgeries

PICTURE TRIVIA

WHO WHAT WHEN & WHERE

5 POINTS per actor — **Who** are the actors in this film?

5 POINTS — **What** is the title of this film?

5 POINTS — **When** was this film released?

5 POINTS — **Who** is the director of this film?

BONUS TRIVIA

10 POINTS — In what (fictional) South American country was Peter Bowman kidnapped by rebels?

10 POINTS — What did the term "the K & R business" stand for?

10 POINTS — How much was the final negotiated price for Bowman's release?

ABOUT THIS MOVIE

Filmed primarily in remote locations in Ecuador, this film benefited from extraordinarily beautiful vistas of rain forests and mountains, but resulted in equally extraordinary inconvenience and hardship. The production crew encountered high-altitude sickness, severe rainstorms replete with hailstones, and even the vestiges of a tear gas dispersion — causing most of the crew to tear up uncontrollably — from a riot that was quelled several blocks away.

Answers • Who? Meg Ryan, Russell Crowe **What?** Proof of Life **When?** 2000 **Who?** Taylor Hackford
Trivia answer 1 Tecala
Trivia answer 2 The kidnap and ransom business
Trivia answer 3 $650,000

PICTURE TRIVIA

WHO WHAT WHEN & WHERE

⑤ **POINTS per actor** **Who** are the actors in this film?

⑤ **POINTS** **What** is the title of this film?

⑤ **POINTS** **When** was this film released?

⑤ **POINTS** **Who** is the director of this film?

BONUS TRIVIA

10 POINTS In what town and state did the filmmakers investigate the legends?

10 POINTS What was the site called where the bodies of five men — mysteriously bound together — were discovered?

10 POINTS Which of the filmmakers (Heather, Josh, and Mike) went missing?

ABOUT THIS MOVIE

With perhaps the exception of the "Star Wars" films, few movies have been the subject of more parodies. This low budget horror movie (shot mostly on video) became a cult hit even before its theatrical release. Innovative filming techniques — a movie shot mostly by the actors themselves — and clever use of online marketing strategies fueled such audience interest that it became a blockbuster success, earning a phenomenal 4,000 times its original production cost.

Answers • Who? Heather Donahue **What?** The Blair Witch Project **When?** 1999 **Who?** Daniel Myrick and Eduardo Sánchez
Trivia answer 1 Burkittsville, Maryland
Trivia answer 2 Coffin Rock
Trivia answer 3 Josh

PICTURE TRIVIA

5 POINTS per actor — **Who** are the actors in this film?

5 POINTS — **What** is the title of this film?

5 POINTS — **When** was this film released?

5 POINTS — **Who** is the director of this film?

BONUS TRIVIA

10 POINTS — What was the name of the U.S. nuclear submarine?

10 POINTS — Which "Defcon" level of emergency did the nuclear crisis reach?

10 POINTS — During the discussion about the war theories of von Clausewitz, what did Lieutenant Commander Hunter consider the "real enemy" in a nuclear world?

ABOUT THIS MOVIE

Suspenseful elements from two very different films came together in this film about a nuclear crisis. An aborted communication in the film "Fail-Safe" failed to turn back a nuclear-armed jet fighter during the Cold War, while an interrupted transmission to the submarine in this film creates an escalating crisis. Also, the hour-long countdown to launch in this film mirrors the near real-time climax of "High Noon."

Answers • Who? Denzel Washington, Gene Hackman **What?** Crimson Tide **When?** 1995 **Who?** Tony Scott
Trivia answer 1 The U.S.S. Alabama
Trivia answer 2 Defcon 3
Trivia answer 3 War itself

PICTURE TRIVIA

WHO WHAT WHEN & WHERE

5 POINTS per actor — **Who** are the actors in this film?

5 POINTS — **What** is the title of this film?

5 POINTS — **When** was this film released?

5 POINTS — **Who** is the director of this film?

BONUS TRIVIA

10 POINTS — What was Keating's favorite motto (in Latin or English)?

10 POINTS — What did Keating tell his class to do with the introduction to the poetry textbook?

10 POINTS — What were the four pillars of education at the Welton Academy prep school?

ABOUT THIS MOVIE

The screenwriter for this film based the main character—an unconventional poetry teacher—on an instructor he knew at his own prep school in Nashville, Tennessee. The original school chosen to appear in the film was in Georgia, but winter scenes were required, and to save on the costs of fake snow, the production was relocated to a school in Delaware.

Answers • Who? Robin Williams **What?** Dead Poets Society **When?** 1989 **Who?** Peter Weir
Trivia answer 1 Carpe Diem (Seize the Day)
Trivia answer 2 Rip it out
Trivia answer 3 Tradition, Honor, Discipline, Excellence

PICTURE TRIVIA

5 POINTS per actor — **Who** are the actors in this film?

5 POINTS — **What** is the title of this film?

5 POINTS — **When** was this film released?

5 POINTS — **Who** is the director of this film?

BONUS TRIVIA

10 POINTS — What did Hoke reveal when he was instructed to find a particular name on a tombstone in the cemetery?

10 POINTS — What game did the ladies always play when they got together over the years?

10 POINTS — What was Hoke's weekly salary raised to after he apprised Boolie of another job offer?

ABOUT THIS MOVIE

Based on a stage play that had already been awarded a Pulitzer, this film's screenplay was also written by the playwright and went on to win a Best Screenplay Oscar — the first time any writer won both awards for the same material.

PICTURE TRIVIA

5 POINTS per actor — **Who** are the actors in this film?

5 POINTS — **What** is the title of this film?

5 POINTS — **When** was this film released?

5 POINTS — **Who** is the director of this film?

BONUS TRIVIA

10 POINTS — What item did Davis purchase in the neighborhood where the murder took place?

10 POINTS — What was between the apartment window of the defendant and the window of the old woman who was the sole eyewitness?

10 POINTS — What was the estimate for how long it took for the old man in the apartment below to reach the stairwell from his bedroom?

ABOUT THIS MOVIE

Despite being shot on a lean production budget ($350,000) in black & white, primarily on a single set (the jury room), and flaunting a sterling cast and compelling story, this film failed to turn a profit at the box office at a time which saw the beginning of the widescreen color extravaganza. But while a commercial failure, it succeeded on all other counts, including starting the career of its first-time feature film director, who would go on to make other now-classic films, such as "The Pawnbroker," "Fail-Safe," and "Serpico."

Answers • Who? Jack Klugman, Edward Binns, Henry Fonda, Ed Begley, E.G. Marshall **What?** Twelve Angry Men **When?** 1957 **Who?** Sidney Lumet
Trivia answer 1 A switch knife nearly identical to the murder weapon presented as evidence in the trial
Trivia answer 2 The elevated train line
Trivia answer 3 41 seconds

PICTURE TRIVIA

WHO WHAT WHEN & WHERE

5 POINTS per actor **Who** are the actors in this film?

5 POINTS **What** is the title of this film?

5 POINTS **When** was this film released?

5 POINTS **Who** is the director of this film?

BONUS TRIVIA

10 POINTS What was the toxic element being introduced into the township's water supply?

10 POINTS What beauty queen title did the lead character once hold?

10 POINTS How many ex-husbands and children did she have?

ABOUT THIS MOVIE

This film follows in the tradition of "Silkwood," "Serpico," "The Insider," and even "All The President's Men," in its depiction of a few individuals prevailing against forces with the power and resources to suppress the truth in favor of their own agendas. True stories of underdogs winning against the odds seem catnip to screenwriters, actors, and directors alike, as all of these films were nominated for Academy Awards in acting, writing, and —with one exception—directing categories in the years they were released.

Answers • Who? Albert Finney, Julia Roberts **What?** Erin Brockovich **When?** 2000 **Who?** Steven Soderbergh
Trivia answer 1 Hexavalent chromium (a.k.a. chromium 6)
Trivia answer 2 Miss Wichita
Trivia answer 3 Two ex-husbands and three children

PICTURE TRIVIA

WHO WHAT WHEN & WHERE

(5) POINTS per actor — **Who** are the actors in this film?

(5) POINTS — **What** is the title of this film?

(5) POINTS — **When** was this film released?

(5) POINTS — **Who** is the director of this film?

BONUS TRIVIA

10 POINTS — What did William Foster's personalized license plate spell?

10 POINTS — What did the park bum find in Foster's briefcase?

10 POINTS — What was the name of the fast food restaurant from which Foster insisted on ordering breakfast after 11:30?

ABOUT THIS MOVIE

The star of this film (which chronicles a day in the life of an ordinary worker who snaps during an oppressive morning commute and simply wants to "go home") wrestled with the nature of the character he was to play right up until he received the conservative, flat-topped crew cut that the character preferred. After that, he felt completely at home in the role.

PICTURE TRIVIA

5 POINTS per actor — **Who** are the actors in this film?

5 POINTS — **What** is the title of this film?

5 POINTS — **When** was this film released?

5 POINTS — **Who** is the director of this film?

BONUS TRIVIA

10 POINTS — Which color pill did Thomas Anderson choose from Morpheus, the blue one or the red one?

10 POINTS — What year did Morpheus estimate it actually was?

10 POINTS — What was the name of the company where Thomas Anderson worked?

ABOUT THIS MOVIE

The now classic "bullet time" and wraparound freeze effects defined the unique look of this film. With only one previous feature under their belts, the two brothers who directed it fused comic book elements, mysticism, philosophy, computer generated imagery, and virtual reality concepts into a groundbreaking experience that can justifiably be described as mind expanding.

Answers • Who? Keanu Reeves, Carrie-Anne Moss **What?** The Matrix **When?** 1999 **Who?** Andy and Larry Wachowski
Trivia answer 1 The red one
Trivia answer 2 Closer to 2199
Trivia answer 3 Metacortex

PICTURE TRIVIA

WHO WHAT WHEN & WHERE

5 POINTS per actor — **Who** are the actors in this film?

5 POINTS — **What** is the title of this film?

5 POINTS — **When** was this film released?

5 POINTS — **Who** is the director of this film?

BONUS TRIVIA

10 POINTS — Where did Frank Slade and Charlie stay while in New York City?

10 POINTS — Which dance did Frank perform with Donna?

10 POINTS — What caliber weapon was Frank Slade's sidearm?

ABOUT THIS MOVIE

After being nominated for Best Actor six times over two decades, a role in this film proved a lucky seventh for its star. As he remarked during his acceptance speech, "You broke my streak!" He was also nominated in two categories — Best Actor and Best Supporting Actor — in the same year, the only male actor to have ever been so nominated.

Answers • Who? Al Pacino, Chris O'Donnell **What?** Scent of a Woman **When?** 1992 **Who?** Martin Brest
Trivia answer 1 The Waldorf-Astoria
Trivia answer 2 The tango
Trivia answer 3 A .45

PICTURETRIVIA

5 POINTS per actor — **Who** are the actors in this film?

5 POINTS — **What** is the title of this film?

5 POINTS — **When** was this film released?

5 POINTS — **Who** is the director of this film?

BONUSTRIVIA

10 POINTS — What was Suzanne's first on-air job at the cable station?

10 POINTS — What was the name of Suzanne's documentary about high school kids?

10 POINTS — Who was Suzanne's dog "Walter" named after?

ABOUT THIS MOVIE

While fictional accounts of ambition and murder are the bedrock for many films, this film was inspired in part by a real-life teacher/student relationship that ended in the murder of the teacher's husband by a young student. The notorious incident took place in New Hampshire, where this film is set.

Answers • Who? Matt Dillon, Nicole Kidman **What?** To Die For **When?** 1995 **Who?** Gus Van Sant
Trivia answer 1 Weather person
Trivia answer 2 "Teens Speak Out!"
Trivia answer 3 Walter Cronkite

PICTURE TRIVIA

5 POINTS per actor — **Who** are the actors in this film?

5 POINTS — **What** is the title of this film?

5 POINTS — **When** was this film released?

5 POINTS — **Who** is the director of this film?

BONUS TRIVIA

10 POINTS — What were the two names for the type of weapon Karl Childers had used?

10 POINTS — What did Karl call the place other people call Hell?

10 POINTS — What gift did Karl give to the boy after he had to move out of the garage?

ABOUT THIS MOVIE

This film began as a black & white short film, the gist of which appears in the interview scene at the beginning of the feature length version. The story of the film's unique and memorable main character was originally developed for the stage. The film's actor/writer/director was nominated for two Oscars — for acting and writing — and won for "Best Adapted Screenplay" even though the story was based on his own earlier versions.

Answers • Who? Dwight Yoakam, Billy Bob Thornton, John Ritter **What?** Sling Blade **When?** 1996 **Who?** Billy Bob Thornton
Trivia answer 1 A kaiser blade or a sling blade
Trivia answer 2 Hades
Trivia answer 3 His stack of books

PICTURE TRIVIA

5 POINTS per actor — **Who** are the actors in this film?

5 POINTS — **What** is the title of this film?

5 POINTS — **When** was this film released?

5 POINTS — **Who** is the director of this film?

BONUS TRIVIA

10 POINTS — How did Oskar get Amon Goeth's servant Helen on the list?

10 POINTS — What three letters indicated the name of Oskar's enamelware factory?

10 POINTS — About how many people made it onto the list?

ABOUT THIS MOVIE

Despite his stature, reputation, and unequaled track record for commercial success, the director of this film still met with strong resistance for his decision to film in black & white. Ultimately, he prevailed, and the film went on to win the Best Picture Oscar and to become the most commercially successful black & white film in cinematic history. And the director took home his first Best Director Oscar as well.

Answers • Who? Ben Kingsley, Liam Neeson **What?** Schindler's List **When?** 1993 **Who?** Steven Spielberg
Trivia answer 1 By winning her from Goeth in a card game of "21"
Trivia answer 2 D.E.F. (Deutsche Emailwaren Fabrique)
Trivia answer 3 1200

All photographs courtesy of the Everett Collection.

While every reasonable effort has been made to correctly acknowledge
the studios credited with the films, GreyCore Press and Picture Trivia IP, LLC.
cannot be held responsible for errors, omissions or inaccuracies.

We welcome any information leading to a more complete acknowledgement
and will include those in any subsequent printing of this book.

CREATOR **Dave Cutler** is an award-winning freelance artist whose images have graced the pages of the nation's leading publications and corporate literature. His first children's book, WHEN I WISHED I WAS ALONE, was published to much acclaim in October 2003. Once a candidate for film school, Dave's love of movies and fascination for moviemaking began as a little boy and continues to this day.

DESIGNER **Beth Crowell** is a principal at Cheung/Crowell Design, a multi-disciplinary graphic design studio in Redding, Connecticut.

RESEARCHER/WRITER **Tony Urgo** is an award-winning screenwriter, playwright, and filmmaker. His plays have been staged in New York City and New Jersey, and his stage adaptation of "Frankenstein" had a successful national tour in the Northeast and Midwest. He made films as a student at New York University and in the production trenches of New Jersey on his own independent feature, "Remembering Maria."

PUBLISHER/EDITOR **Joan Schweighardt** is the president of GreyCore Press, which has earned a reputation for continuously publishing titles that are "delightfully offbeat."

3 MEN AND A BABY • Buena Vista Pictures • Touchstone Pictures

48 HOURS • Paramount Pictures

A BEAUTIFUL MIND • Imagine Entertainment • Universal Pictures

A FEW GOOD MEN • Castle Rock Entertainment • Columbia Pictures • New Line Cinema

A FISH CALLED WANDA • Metro-Goldwyn-Mayer

A STAR IS BORN • Warner Bros.

A STREETCAR NAMED DESIRE • Warner Bros.

ABSENCE OF MALICE • Columbia Pictures • Mirage Productions

AIRPLANE! • Paramount Pictures

ALMOST FAMOUS • DreamWorks SKG • Vinyl Films

AMERICAN BEAUTY • DreamWorks • Jinks/Cohen Company

AMERICAN GRAFFITI • Lucasfilm Ltd. • The Coppola Company • Universal Pictures

AN OFFICER AND A GENTLEMAN • Lorimar Film Entertainment • Paramount Pictures

ANNIE HALL • Rollins-Joffe Productions • United Artists

APOCALYPSE NOW • United Artists • Zoetrope Studios

AS GOOD AS IT GETS • Gracie Films • TriStar Pictures

AWAKENINGS • Columbia Pictures

BASIC INSTINCT • Carolco • Le Studio Canal+ • TriStar

BEETLEJUICE • Geffen Pictures • Warner Bros.

BEN-HUR • Metro-Goldwyn-Mayer

BILLY ELLIOT • Arts Council of England • BBC • Le Studio Canal+ • Tiger Aspect Productions
    USA Films • WT2 • Working Title Films

BLADE RUNNER • The Ladd Company • Warner Bros.

BLOW • Avery Pix • New Line Cinema • Spanky Pictures

BONNIE AND CLYDE • Tatira-Hiller Productions • Warner Bros./Seven Arts

BRIDGET JONES'S DIARY • Little Bird Ltd. • Le Studio Canal+ • Miramax Films • Working Title Films

BUGSY • Baltimore Pictures • Desert Vision • Mulholland Productions • TriStar Pictures

BULL DURHAM • The Mount Company • Orion Pictures

CASABLANCA • Warner Bros.

CAT ON A HOT TIN ROOF • Avon Productions • Metro-Goldwyn-Mayer

CHILDREN OF A LESSER GOD • Paramount Pictures

CHINATOWN • Paramount Pictures

CITIZEN KANE • Mercury Productions • RKO Radio Pictures

CITY SLICKERS • Castle Rock Entertainment • Columbia Pictures Nelson Entertainment

CLOSE ENCOUNTERS OF THE THIRD KIND • Columbia Pictures

CRIMSON TIDE • Simpson/Bruckheimer • Hollywood Films

DEAD POETS SOCIETY • Touchstone • Silver Screen Partners IV • Buena Vista Pictures

DELIVERANCE • Warner Bros.

DICK TRACY • Buena Vista Pictures • Mulholland Productions • Touchstone Pictures

DINER • Metro-Goldwyn-Mayer

DIRTY HARRY • The Malpaso Company • Warner Bros.

DRIVING MISS DAISY • Majestic Films International • The Zanuck Company • Warner Brothers

DUCK SOUP • Paramount Pictures

DUMB AND DUMBER • Motion Picture Corporation of America • New Line Cinema

ERIN BROCKOVICH • Jersey Films • Universal

FAIL-SAFE • Columbia Pictures

FALLING DOWN • Alcor Films • Le Studio Canal • Regency Enterprises • Warner Bros.

FAR AND AWAY • Imagine Entertainment • Universal Pictures

FATAL ATTRACTION • Paramount Pictures

FATHER GOOSE • Universal Pictures

FERRIS BUELLER'S DAY OFF • Paramount Pictures

FIELD OF DREAMS • Gordon Company • Universal Pictures

FORREST GUMP • Brooksfilms Ltd. • Paramount Pictures

GOOD MORNING VIETNAM • Buena Vista Pictures • Touchstone Pictures

GOOD WILL HUNTING • Lawrence Bender Productions • Miramax Films

GOODFELLAS • Warner Bros.

GROUNDHOG DAY • Columbia Pictures

GUESS WHO'S COMING TO DINNER • Columbia Pictures

HEAVEN CAN WAIT • Paramount Pictures

KLUTE • Warner Bros.

KRAMER VS. KRAMER • Columbia Pictures

L.A. CONFIDENTIAL • Regency Enterprises • Warner Bros.

LETHAL WEAPON 2 • Silver Pictures • Warner Bros.

LIFE WITH FATHER • Warner Bros.

LOVE STORY • Paramount Pictures

MARATHON MAN • Paramount Pictures

MEET THE PARENTS • DreamWorks SKG • Nancy Tenenbaum Productions
Tribeca Productions • Universal Pictures

MEN IN BLACK • Amblin Entertainment • Columbia Pictures

MIDNIGHT COWBOY • Jerome Hellman Productions • United Artists

MIDNIGHT EXPRESS • Casablanca Filmworks • Columbia Pictures

MISERY • Castle Rock Entertainment • Columbia Pictures • Nelson Entertainment

MISSION: IMPOSSIBLE • Cruise-Wagner Productions • Paramount Pictures

MISTER ROBERTS • Warner Bros.

MOONSTRUCK • Metro-Goldwyn-Mayer

MR. SMITH GOES TO WASHINGTON • Columbia Pictures

MYSTIC PIZZA • Samuel Goldwyn Company

NOTORIOUS • RKO Radio Pictures

O BROTHER, WHERE ART THOU? • Buena Vista Pictures • Mike Zoss Productions
    Le Studio Canal+ • Touchstone Pictures • Universal Pictures • Working Title Films

ONE FLEW OVER THE CUCKOO'S NEST • Fantasy Films • United Artists

PAPER MOON • Paramount Pictures

PAPILLON • Allied Artists Solar Productions

PEE WEE'S BIG ADVENTURE • Warner Bros.

PEGGY SUE GOT MARRIED • Delphi V Productions • TriStar Pictures • Zoetrope Studios

PILLOW TALK • Arwin Productions • Universal International Pictures

PLEASANTVILLE • Larger Than Life Productions • New Line Cinema

POLTERGEIST • Metro-Goldwyn-Mayer

PRETTY WOMAN • Buena Vista Pictures • Touchstone Pictures

PROOF OF LIFE • Anvil Films • Bel Air Entertainment • Castle Rock Entertainment • Warner Bros.

PULP FICTION • A Band Apart • Jersey Films • Miramax Films

QUIZ SHOW • Baltimore Pictures • Buena Vista Pictures • Hollywood Pictures • Wildwood Enterprises

RAGING BULL • Chartoff-Winkler Productions • United Artists

RAIDERS OF THE LOST ARK /Lucasfilm Ltd. • Paramount Pictures

RAIN MAN • Guber-Peters Company • Mirage Entertainment • United Artists

ROCKY • Chartoff-Winkler Productions • United Artists

ROSEMARY'S BABY • Paramount Pictures

SATURDAY NIGHT FEVER • Paramount Pictures • Robert Stigwood Organization

SAVING PRIVATE RYAN • Amblin Entertainment • DreamWorks SKG

   Mark Gordon Productions • Mutual Film Company • Paramount Pictures

SCENT OF A WOMAN • Universal • City Light Pictures

SCHINDLER'S LIST • Amblin Entertainment • Universal

SERPICO • Paramount Pictures

SHAKESPEARE IN LOVE • Bedford Falls Productions • Miramax Films • Universal Pictures

SLEEPLESS IN SEATTLE • TriStar Pictures

SLING BLADE • The Shooting Gallery • Miramax

STRIPES • Columbia Pictures

TAXI DRIVER • Bill/Phillips • Columbia Pictures

TERMS OF ENDEARMENT • Paramount Pictures

THE AMERICAN PRESIDENT • Castle Rock Enterntainment • Columbia Pictures

   Universal Pictures • Wildwood Enterprises

THE BIRDCAGE • Metro-Goldwyn-Mayer • United Artists

THE BISHOP'S WIFE • RKO Radio Pictures • Samuel Goldwyn Company

THE BLAIR WITCH PROJECT • Haxan Films • Artisan Entertainment

THE BRIDGE ON THE RIVER KWAI • Columbia Pictures • Horizon Pictures

THE CAINE MUTINY • Columbia Pictures

THE CHINA SYNDROME • Columbia Pictures • IPC Films

THE CIDER HOUSE RULES • Film Colony • Miramax Films

THE CRYING GAME • British Screen • Channel Four Films • Miramax

THE DEER HUNTER • EMI Films Ltd. • Universal Pictures

THE DIRTY DOZEN • Metro-Goldwyn-Mayer • Seven Arts Productions

THE ELEPHANT MAN • Paramount Pictures

THE FRESHMAN • TriStar Pictures

THE FUGITIVE • Warner Bros.

THE GRADUATE • Embassy Pictures • Lawrence Turman

THE GUNS OF NAVARONE • Columbia Pictures • Open Road

THE LORD OF THE RINGS: THE RETURN OF THE KING • New Line Cinema

   The Saul Zaentz Company • Wingnut Films

THE MALTESE FALCON • First National Pictures • Warner Bros.

THE MASK • Dark Horse Entertainment • New Line Cinema

THE MATRIX • Warner Brothers • Silver Pictures • Village Roadshow Pictures

THE ODD COUPLE • Paramount Pictures

THE PHILADELPHIA STORY • Metro-Goldwyn-Mayer

THE QUIET MAN • Argosy Productions • Republic Pictures

THE RIGHT STUFF • The Ladd Company • Warner Bros.

THE SHAWSHANK REDEMPTION • Castle Rock Entertainment • Columbia Pictures

THE SHINING • Hawk Films Ltd. • Warner Bros.

THE STING • Universal Pictures

WHOWHATWHEN&WHERE

THE TERMINATOR • Cinema 84 • Euro Film Fund Hemdale Film • Pacific Western

THE THOMAS CROWN AFFAIR • Irish Dreamtime • United Artists

THE UNTOUCHABLES • Paramount Pictures

THE USUAL SUSPECTS • Bad Hat Harry Productions • Blue Parrot • Gramercy Pictures
   Polygram Filmed Entertainment • Spelling Films International

THE WITCHES OF EASTWICK • Guber-Peters Company • Kennedy Miller Productions • Warner Bros.

THELMA & LOUISE • Metro-Goldwyn-Mayer • Pathé Entertainment

TO CATCH A THIEF • Paramount Pictures

TO DIE FOR • Columbia • The Rank Organization

TOOTSIE • Columbia Pictures • Punch Productions

TOP GUN • Paramount Pictures

TWELVE ANGRY MEN • Orion-Nova Productions • United Artists

UNBREAKABLE • Blinding Edge Pictures • Buena Vista Pictures • Touchstone Pictures

VANILLA SKY • Artisan Entertainment • Cruise-Wagner Productions • Paramount Pictures • Vinyl Films

WAYNE'S WORLD • Paramount Pictures

WEST SIDE STORY • Mirisch Films • Seven Arts Productions • United Artists

WESTWORLD • Metro-Goldwyn-Mayer

WHEN HARRY MET SALLY • Castle Rock Entertainment • Columbia Pictures • Nelson Entertainment

WHITE CHRISTMAS • Paramount Pictures

YOU'VE GOT MAIL • Warner Bros.